"In telling the story of how the Alaska Native Brotherhood saved Alaska aboriginal rights from being eliminated during the Alaska statehood era, Peter Metcalfe reclaims an important, and until now, overlooked contribution by our organization and that of the Alaska Native Sisterhood in shaping the Alaska we know today."
  —William Martin, Grand President of the Alaska Native Brotherhood

"This is a fascinating look into the role of Southeast Alaska Natives at a critical time in Alaska's history. These are exactly the types of stories we hoped the Alaska Statehood Experience program would capture."
  —Diane Kaplan, President, Rasmuson Foundation

"It is amazing how well those who came before us organized politically to achieve so much—the right to vote, equal education, the anti-discrimination act, and then saving Alaska Native claims. As this book proves, without the ANB/ANS, there would have been no Alaska Native Claims Settlement Act. This is an inspiring story, a part of Alaska's history we should all know."
  —Ethel Lund, member of the ANB/ANS
  Grand Camp Executive Committee

"The ANB/ANS played critically important roles in our contemporary history as Alaska Native people. I am delighted to see serious research and writing about the contributions of the ANB/ANS to all Alaskans. My father-in-law, Herman Kitka Sr., was an ANB member for over sixty years. He took great pride in his ANB membership and in the organization's many accomplishments. This book is an important new contribution to the history of Alaska."
  —Julie Kitka, President, Alaska Federation of Natives

T0308906

"In *A Dangerous Idea*, Peter Metcalfe provides significant and badly needed insight into a missing chapter in the story of Alaska statehood. While Territorial Governor Ernest Gruening and Territorial Congressional Delegate Bob Bartlett were sympathetic toward Native rights, both were ready to put those rights aside if they impeded Alaska's economic development or threatened the success of the statehood movement.

"Leaders of the Alaska Native Brotherhood, which had fought for decades to win recognition of Native rights and dignity, determined that the organization could not support statehood without guarantees that Natives claims would be respected and a legal opportunity provided for their fair hearing. The ANB insisted on including Section 4 in the statehood act by which Alaskans disclaimed title to all land and resources that may be subject to Native claims. Its inclusion is a testament to the vision, determination, and power of the ANB, and the commitment of ANB leaders.

"Metcalfe's fully documented explanation of that commitment and the ANB's success is a long overdue component of any complete understanding of the extraordinary saga of Alaska's remarkable campaign for statehood."

—Stephen Haycox, Professor of History,
University of Alaska Anchorage

A Dangerous Idea

A Dangerous Idea

The Alaska Native Brotherhood
and the Struggle for Indigenous Rights

Peter Metcalfe

with Kathy Kolkhorst Ruddy

University of Alaska Press
Fairbanks

University of Alaska Press
P.O. Box 756240
Fairbanks, AK 99775-6240

Library of Congress Cataloging-in-Publication Data
Metcalfe, Peter, 1951–
    A dangerous idea : the Alaska Native Brotherhood and the struggle for indigenous rights / Peter Metcalfe.
        pages cm
    Includes bibliographical references.
    ISBN 978-1-60223-239-6 (paperback : alkaline paper) — ISBN 978-1-60223-240-2 (electronic)
    1. Alaska Natives—Civil rights—History—20th century. 2. Alaska Native Brotherhood—History. 3. Alaska Natives—Land tenure—History—20th century. 4. Alaska Natives—Government relations—History—20th century. 5. Alaska Natives—Claims—History—20th century. 6. United States. Alaska Native Claims Settlement Act. 7. Alaska—Ethnic relations—History—20th century. I. Title.
    E78.A3M47 2014
    323.1197'0798—dc23
                            2014011901

Cover design: Publishers' Design and Production Services, Inc.
Cover photo: The carvings that top the totem pole named *Honoring Those Who Give* represent members of the Alaska Native Sisterhood and Alaska Native Brotherhood. The thirty-foot pole was carved in the late 1990s by Tlingit artist Nathan Jackson, with assistance from Fred Trout and Donny Varnell, and erected in Ketchikan, Alaska. Photo by Hall Anderson.

This publication was printed on acid-free paper that meets the minimum requirements for ANSI / NISO Z39.48–1992 (R2002) (Permanence of Paper for Printed Library Materials).

Printed in the United States

Dedicated to the memory of

Andrew "Andy" Hope III

It was Andy Hope's idea to write the Rasmuson Foundation/Alaska Humanities Forum grant that funded the research for this project. Tragically, during the summer of 2008 when the grant was awarded, Andy was diagnosed with an aggressive form of cancer. He died six weeks later. Both the author and the researcher were Andy's close friends and colleagues over many years, when we each worked with Andy on publications and on radio and video projects, all of which involved Tlingit and Haida history, culture, and language. Like his father, Andrew "John" Hope, and grandfather, Andrew Percy Hope, Andy left behind a powerful legacy. Of relevance to the Statehood Experience Grant were the historical records he had compiled over a lifetime of research, which he left in the care of the author—about thirty file boxes—that provided documentation referenced in this book.

Contents

Foreword ix

Preface xiii

Introduction xix

1. Aboriginal Title in Alaska 1

2. The Alaska Native Brotherhood 13

3. Suing the Government 35

4. Reservations in Alaska 45

5. A Bad Time for Indians 57

6. The Extinguishment Legislation 65

7. Statehood or Native Claims 75

8. Shaping Alaska 87

Notes 91

References 121

Cases Cited 124

About the Author and Researchers 125

Index 127

Foreword

The first year and first month of law school introduced me to the concept of "sword and shield." Justice could thrive when there existed the "sword" of litigation to advance good ideas and the "shield" of defense against bad or unfair ideas. The battle played out in the courts as well as in the legislative branch.

Although the original title of this book, "The Sword and the Shield," was not possible because of the release of another book of identical title, the battle imagery is apt for the sustained civil rights struggle Peter Metcalfe is describing. *A Dangerous Idea* captures the passion and courage of this history.

The Alaska Native Brotherhood (ANB), now 102 years old, took up the litigation sword and the shield of congressional committee room debate for aboriginal title in the 1930s with only one professionally trained attorney—William Paul Sr. of Wrangell.

Paul's incessant letters, distributed through word of mouth, the mimeograph machine, and pages-thick carbon paper, electrified the Southeast Native population, and many other leaders stepped forward to join the battle.

When Paul was first elected grand secretary of the ANB in 1920 in the territory of Alaska, Native people were not citizens, could not vote unless white people testified that they were "civilized," and could not own real property or hold territorial licenses. "No Natives" signs limited Native participation in the white society and economy.

Would the Americans follow their own Constitution when these injustices were presented? "Equal protection" and "due process" are strong words, but insignificant if they are not effectively presented to the government. It was Alice Walker who wrote that the most common way people give up power is by thinking that they do not have any.

In the summer of 1977, I arrived in Juneau as a law clerk to then–Chief Justice Robert Boochever of the Alaska Supreme Court, eager to reconnect with the infant state where I had lived in U. S. Coast Guard family quarters in Kodiak for two years before the 1959 statehood. Throughout my subsequent work in the attorney general's office, and then years in private practice, I was intrigued by the puzzle of aboriginal title in Alaska. Did it really exist? If so, what did it mean? What had really happened to aboriginal title at statehood? Had the rule of law prevailed or not? What inspired the Southeast Alaska Natives to take up the sword and shield to see if the American sense of justice would include them?

The opportunity to track down the meaning of these questions appeared when the Rasmuson Foundation funded the Alaska Statehood Experience grants through the Alaska Humanities Forum in 2009. After fifty years, it was time to redefine statehood while many participants were still alive. It was a sad honor, after Andy Hope's untimely death, to carry forward the historical and legal evaluation of aboriginal title in Alaska in a grant authored by Andy and by Peter Metcalfe.

Other questions that were asked during the research by Peter, myself, and other members of our team were: Exactly what did the United States receive when it signed the Treaty of Cession with, and paid cash to, the Russians? How did Alaska differ from other expansions of federal authority into lands occupied by Native Americans, and why had there been no treaties with Alaska Natives?

Peter Metcalfe's sharp analysis, painstaking research, and approachable narrative style in this book open a world into this era as we, thanks to this visionary Rasmuson contribution, rethink Alaska statehood in a mature context. The first fifty years of statehood history are often steeped in Alaska exceptionalism and frequently lacking in mention of aboriginal people. It has been a pleasure to assist Peter in redefining the next phase of Alaska statehood historical review.

The time frame of this book's focus—1945 to 1958—starts twenty-one years after citizenship was extended to Native peoples in the United States. And while Alaska Natives became citizens, their status as Native Americans remained unique: there had been no recognition or resolution of their indigenous rights. No military defeat, no treaties defined their status.

How did our Constitution measure up when faced with a first people who organized and stood up for those rights so eloquently written into this foundational American document? Would Alaska Natives receive the protections they were due in American constitutional law?

Read this book and see for yourself. And if you are inspired by this history of courage and perseverance, please tell someone else, and especially teach it to a child.

Kathy Kolkhorst Ruddy
July 2014

Rosita Worl (left), head of the Sealaska Heritage Institute; Nathan Jackson (center), a renowned artist; and Marcello Quinto (right), former director of Goldbelt, an Alaska Native urban corporation, are of the generation of Alaska Native leaders who came of age in the years following Alaska statehood. They appear here in their clan regalia participating in the entrance parade of Celebration 2008. Photo by Peter Metcalfe.

Preface

This book began with the receipt of a research grant from the Alaska Humanities Forum's Alaska Statehood Experience program, which was funded by the Rasmuson Foundation to celebrate the fiftieth anniversary of Alaska statehood. The stated purpose of the grant we submitted was to determine the level of Alaska Native participation in the Alaska statehood movement.

During the research phase of our project, we could find no evidence of organized involvement in the statehood issue by Alaska Natives except for the Alaska Native Brotherhood, which stood united in opposition to any statehood proposal that might have undermined aboriginal claims. As we pursued this line of research, it became apparent that the ANB's success in protecting those claims during the years leading up to statehood was an achievement that strongly influenced the subsequent development of the state of Alaska. We also found that this contribution to Alaska's history had been overlooked.

To fully understand the ANB's achievement, we documented the early efforts by the ANB leaders to establish the basis for pursuing aboriginal claims, the development of two lawsuits that sought redress in the U.S. Court of Claims, and the organization's campaign during the years of the statehood movement to protect the claims being tested in court from efforts in Congress to either eliminate Alaska Native claims altogether or to brush them aside with a quick and cheap settlement.

The results of our research were published in 2010 as an essay, "The Sword and the Shield." With the thought of honoring the hundredth anniversary of the Alaska Native Brotherhood, established in 1912, we chose to republish in a book format, now titled *A Dangerous Idea*. We added photographs and illustrations throughout and also took the opportunity to make extensive additions and revisions, enough so that the original essay can be considered a rough draft.

In referencing this period, we have endeavored to present contemporary points of view without the distortion of present-day perspectives. One result of this may seem to diminish the importance of the Alaska Native Sisterhood. Insofar as we could determine, ANS members were deeply involved in the issues of the day, and their advice solicited and respected by the ANB membership, but, with a few exceptions, the contributions of women remained in the background.

We were fortunate to have had access to private correspondence and documents from the family of William Paul Sr., as well as records collected by our late colleague Andy Hope that included transcripts of government hearings, newspaper articles and histories of the period, unpublished manuscripts and academic papers, and various publications. Thanks to our team we were able to tap sources that could otherwise have been found only through the most fortuitous of circumstances. Obscure records were contributed by Stephen Langdon, who also conducted interviews, and Kathy Kolkhorst Ruddy, who, in addition to her research of legal records, secured and arranged for the preservation, in digital format, of interviews by the late Vern Metcalfe (the author's father) with Native leaders recorded in 1987 to commemorate the seventy-fifth anniversary of the Alaska Native Brotherhood.

In the months before we completed the essay, reviewers of our rough drafts challenged the factual basis of several assertions. Where appropriate, we made changes; otherwise we defended our position, and in those cases the disagreements are set forth in the endnotes. But at no time during the review, nor since we published and distributed the essay, has anyone attacked the central premise: that without the Alaska Native Brotherhood there would have been few if any Native claims to settle after Alaska became a state.

The editorial "we" of this preface is more than a convention. *A Dangerous Idea* is the product of a team effort. Without the research and legal analysis of Kathy Kolkhorst Ruddy and, more important, the discussions her findings inspired, it is unlikely that we would have been able to reveal and put into perspective the hitherto-forgotten accomplishment of the ANB in protecting Native claims.

A key member of our team, Stephen Langdon, professor and chair of the Department of Anthropology (retired), University of Alaska Anchorage, served as our project adviser. His deep knowledge of the subjects we covered, his resources and interview skills, and his challenges of early drafts all contributed to the content. We acknowledge Liz Dodd's copyediting skills and the help and contributions of my sister, Kim Metcalfe, both for her research on behalf of this project and for her book, *In Sisterhood,* which is referenced.

The collective work of Richard and Nora Dauenhauer informed this project. The Dauenhauers are also principals of Tlingit Readers Inc., a nonprofit they founded along with the late Andy Hope. The Alaska Humanities Forum awarded the grant that funded this project to Tlingit Readers, and Richard served as our grant administrator.

The Alaska Arts and Humanities Foundation research grant might not have been approved were it not for the support provided by Cathy Muñoz of Juneau, a member of the review committee. We also very much appreciated the technical assistance we received from Laura Schue of the foundation—she was as kind as she was helpful and attentive.

We gratefully recognize the assistance, time, and hospitality afforded by Ben Paul, son of Bill Paul Jr., in providing access to his father's and grandfather's personal files. We also thank Frances Paul DeGermain, William Paul Sr.'s daughter, for granting an interview and providing access to her father's records. And we acknowledge the help provided by the staffs of the Sealaska Heritage Institute and the Alaska State Historical Library.

In addition to our project advisor, Professor Langdon, reviewers of the early drafts of this work included Wallace Olson, professor of anthropology (emeritus), University of Alaska Southeast; Robert Price, retired federal solicitor and former ANCSA corporate attorney; and Donald Craig Mitchell, ANCSA historian and former attorney for the Alaska Federation of Natives. Stephen Haycox, professor of history, University of Alaska Anchorage, provided access to an early unpublished paper ("Promises and Denouement") and much encouragement. We thank all of them for offering comments, which resulted in many improvements.

Delegates to the 1929 ANB/ANS Grand Camp convention, Haines, Alaska. Photo courtesy of the Andrew Hope III collection.

No identification key is known to exist for the ANS women in attendance at the 1929 convention. Photo courtesy of the Andrew Hope III collection.

Row G
Row F
Row E
Row D
Row C
Row B
Row A

Row A
1. Andrew Hope Sr.
2. Sandy Stevens
3. George Demmert
4. Charles Newton
5. W. L. Paul Sr.
6. Louis F. Paul
7. Frank Price
8. George Ward
9. Ralph Young Sr.

Row B
10. Sam Davis
11. John Ward
12. George Haldane
13. Johnnie Hanson
14. Albert Kookesh
15. Peter Simpson
16. Ray James Sr.
17. Edward Marshall
18. James Fox
19. Jack Ellis
20. Charlie Jones

Row C
21. Jim Stevens
22. Bill Brady
23. Mark Jacobs Sr.
24. Ray James Sr.
25. George Betts
26. Sam Johnson
27. Sam Martin
28. Haines Dewitt
29. unknown
30. James Brown
31. Frank Mercer
32. Frank G. Johnson

Row D
33. unknown
34. James D. Jackson
35. Ed Warren
36. Rudolph Walton
37. Shorty Johnson
38. George Williams
39. James Klanott
40. unknown
41. David Howard
42. Sam Jackson
43. unknown
44. John Marks Thlunaut
45. unknown

Row E
46. unknown
47. unknown
48. Seward Kunz
49. Arthur Johnson
50. Frank Peratrovich
51. Cecil Nix
52. Joseph Allen
53. unknown
54. John Shorty
55. Leo Dennis
56. unknown
57. Sam Dennis
58. Joe Wright
59. James Willard

Row F
60. unknown
61. Mathew Lawrence
62. Gus Klaney
63. John Benson
64. Frank S. James
65. Fritz Willard
66. Frank Jimmie
67. John David
68. Steve Perrin
69. unknown
70. unknown
71. Patsy Davis
72. unknown

Row G
73. unknown
74. James Lee
75. Henry Brown
76. Thomas Andrews
77. Bill Johnson
78. Tom Johnson
79. John Jackson
80. Jack David
81. unknown
82. Tom Jimmie
83. Charlie James
84. Dave Klanott
85. Chief John Donanak
86. Jimmie Young
87. unknown
88. Mr. Young
89. Harry Williams
90. unknown
91. James Watson

Peter Metcalfe prepared this identification key in collaboration with Judson Brown in 1981. In addition to Judson Brown, among those standing in the back are James Clark, Ben Watson, Andrew Johnson, Jerry Williams, James Martin, Sergius Sheakley, Willie Williams, Charles Anderson, Johnnie Willard, Robert Perkins, and Chauncy Jacobs. In his book Brothers in Harmony, *David P. Light named the following as also present: Alfred Andrews, Peter Brown, Paddy Goenett, Andrew Jackson, and Sam Jacobs.*

On a personal note, I wish to acknowledge the inspiration and insights I have received from my Alaska Native friends and colleagues, including, in no particular order, Marie Olson, Carlton Smith, Richard George, Bill Martin, Walter Johns, Andy Ebona, David Katzeek, Marcello Quinto, Selina Everson, Joaqlin Estus, Sam Demmert, Gordon Jackson, Harold Martin, Mike Jackson, Ruth Demmert, Byron Mallott, and the late Cyril George Sr., Ivan Gamble, Walter Porter, Justin Brown, and Reverend Dr. Walter Soboleff. I doubt I would have had the confidence to tackle this subject without the support of the family of my late friend and mentor, Andy Hope, or the encouragement and insights provided by Frank O. Williams and Ethel Lund, who served as Grand Camp presidents (ANB and ANS, respectively) and remain active members of the Grand Camp executive committee.

I credit my late father, Vern Metcalfe, for paving the way. It was he who forged my family's lasting connections and abiding friendships with so many Alaska Natives.

Thanks are also due to my dear wife, Sandy, for her patience, support, and tolerance of the time I devoted to this project.

Peter Metcalfe
July 2014

Introduction

During the post-World War II era, the Alaska Native Brotherhood positioned itself as a serious obstacle in the path of the Alaska statehood movement. ANB leaders were determined to protect the aboriginal claims they were testing in court from politically powerful interests that sought to eliminate or minimize those claims as a price for the admission of Alaska to the Union.

Few political leaders in the post-war era gave much credence to the aboriginal rights of Alaska Natives. During the formative years of the Alaska Native Brotherhood (1912–1929), even some of its members had doubts, believing that the concept of aboriginal rights was a "dangerous idea," one that might compromise their collective efforts to win the full benefits of U.S. citizenship.

In his single-volume history of Alaska, Stephen Haycox, an American cultural historian with the University of Alaska Anchorage, describes the Alaska Native Brotherhood as the "only viable Native organization in the territory before statehood."[1] The ANB's structure and cadre of educated leaders, aided by the fund-raising prowess of the Alaska Native Sisterhood,[2] gave it the capability to effectively combat the interests arrayed against them.

Alaska Natives were not without friends and allies. Organizations such as the National Congress of American Indians and the Association on American Indian Affairs came to their defense at crucial junctures. While these efforts helped, the first ten years following World War II proved to be a time of great peril for Native American interests in general, and those of Alaska Natives in particular. During this period, even

Alaska's highest-ranking political leaders—Governor Ernest Gruening and the territory's sole congressional delegate, E. L. "Bob" Bartlett, both sympathetic to Alaska Natives and supportive of compensation for lost aboriginal rights—showed little enthusiasm for broader Native claims, especially when perceived to be in conflict with their top political priority: statehood.

In retrospect, it is worth considering one of the great what-ifs of Alaska history: what would Alaska look like today if aboriginal claims had been eliminated or settled prior to statehood? It is not difficult to imagine that with no Native claims to be addressed there would have been no grand settlement like the Alaska Native Claims Settlement Act (ANCSA) passed by Congress in 1971, and, of great significance to Natives and non-Natives alike, without ANCSA there would have been no Section 17(d)(2) by which eighty million acres of Alaska land was set aside for future consideration as national park, wilderness, or other protective designations. This section—known as "d-2"—ignited the Alaska lands battle of the late 1970s, culminating in the Alaska National Interest Lands Conservation Act (ANILCA) of 1980, which, among other provisions, more than doubled the total acreage in the United States under permanent protection.

Counterfactual what-ifs can be far-fetched, but in the case of Native claims there are some near certainties: had Congress settled Native claims prior to statehood, then the legal obstacle of aboriginal title would have been removed, clearing the way for the oil industry to acquire the rights-of-way needed in the 1970s to build the Trans-Alaska Pipeline. Few who have studied Alaska Native claims would deny that clearing the pipeline's path of prior claims provided the motive to settle and that the support of an oil industry eager to attain access to the resource was key to the size of the settlement in dollars and land. And in regards to what came next—the Alaska National Interest Lands Conservation Act— few knowledgeable students of that legislation would deny that absent Section 17(d)(2) of ANCSA, any such effort to protect huge swaths of wilderness areas in Alaska would have been delayed and then severely hobbled by national political realignments that followed the election of Ronald Reagan as president.[3]

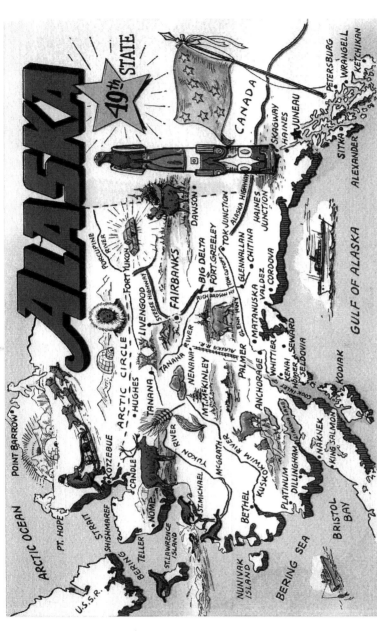

The Alaska Statehood Act conveyed to the new state selection rights to 104 million acres but also included a provision, Section 4 (the "Disclaimer Clause"), that recognized the right and title of Alaska Natives to any lands or other property (including fishing rights) subject to claims, and reserved to the federal government the responsibility of resolving questions of ownership. Ignoring Section 4, the new state began to impose onerous restrictions on hunting and fishing and began selecting lands regardless of Alaska Native use and occupancy. These actions prompted, in 1966, the formation of the Alaska Federation of Natives, which proceeded to lobby for a statewide settlement of Native claims.

ANCSA represents a huge social experiment, the benefits and consequences of which remain a source of lingering dispute. Departing from the
land-reservation paradigm that controlled the aboriginal claims of Native
Americans in the Lower 48, in ANCSA Congress fashioned a settlement
based on a corporate model of privately held equity rather than common
property held in perpetual trust by the U.S. government. In exchange for
money and title to huge tracts of land conveyed to private, Native-owned,
for-profit corporations, all Native claims were extinguished.[4] Congress
imposed the settlement by legislative fiat.[5] There was no referendum by
which Alaska Natives could weigh the costs and benefits and then vote for
or against the settlement.

The corporate model proved to be an awkward fit and, for many Alaska
Native groups, a culturally inappropriate method to effect a Native claims
settlement. Yet it was through ANCSA that Alaska Natives gained the
political power that comes with the financial strength embodied in the
twelve regional corporations and more than two hundred village corporations created under the terms of the act.[6] The Alaska Federation of
Natives, organized in 1966 to lead the Alaska Native claims effort and,

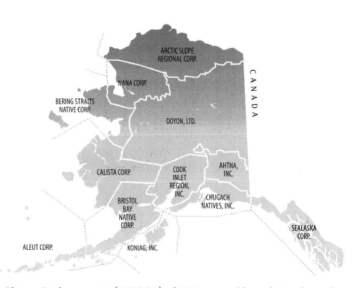

*The Alaska Native Claims Settlement Act (ANCSA) of 1971 created boundaries for twelve
regional corporations that loosely encompassed the ethnological subdivisions of Alaska's
indigenous peoples. Village and urban corporations were also organized, more than two
hundred in all. The combined economic power of the ANCSA corporations leveraged major
changes in the social and political life of the state. By Sue Kraft/courtesy of Peter Metcalfe.*

since the settlement, financially supported by ANCSA corporations, is today one of the most powerful lobbying interests in Alaska.[7]

The Alaska Native Brotherhood can justly take pride that its leadership overcame the reluctance of some members to sue the government and, through the sword of litigation (*Tee-Hit-Ton Indians v. United States* and *Tlingit and Haida Indians of Alaska v. United States*), proved the validity of aboriginal title in Alaska.[8] While important, these cases would have been rendered moot had Congress adopted any one of several prestatehood proposals hostile to Alaska Native interests. The shield that was deployed by the ANB and its allies during those legislative maneuvers protected aboriginal rights in Alaska. Had the ANB failed in either court or Congress, there would have been few, if any, claims left to settle after statehood and, therefore, no Alaska Native Claims Settlement Act.

In the eighteenth century Europeans commonly believed that lands not claimed through some previous act of possession by another "civilized" power were terra nullius—*land belonging to no one.*

1

Aboriginal Title in Alaska

In the history of Alaska, it would be difficult to find a more uncertain legal concept that had greater consequence than aboriginal title.[9] Unlike the circumstances that prevailed in the continental United States, there had been neither formal military actions against nor treaties with Alaska Natives. Instead, in the years following the Treaty of Cession with Russia in 1867, the United States simply expropriated Alaska Native property as if it were not owned by anyone.

The Western legal theory of aboriginal title, often referred to as "Indian title," holds that by right of "discovery" or conquest a sovereign power was entitled to control all the lands under its dominion. This theory (in the United States, an extension of British law and custom) recognized aboriginal title as distinct from fee simple, or private title. According to U.S. constitutional law, worked out in a series of Supreme Court decisions[10] in the early nineteenth century, aboriginal title conferred the rights of use and occupancy, and only Congress could extinguish these rights. Land held in common by a tribe could only be ceded to, or by, the federal government. A tribe could not sell land to a state or to private individuals, nor could states or private interests claim, purchase, or otherwise take land subject to aboriginal title.

Tribes were designated "domestic dependent nations" subject to the supremacy clause of the U.S. Constitution. In other words, a tribe has sovereignty on its own land except when superseded by federal law.

In regards to Alaska, with the exception of the Tsimshians on Annette Island, Congress had not formally recognized any tribes. Without such recognition, could there be aboriginal title? It was a question that would perplex those who were to consider aboriginal title during the statehood era.

1

Throughout this book, *extinguish* is used in the context of a federal process that cancels an aboriginal claim in return for compensation or other considerations. As will be described, Congress contemplated various drafts of legislation during the Alaska statehood era that would have eliminated those claims without compensation.

From the founding of the United States, extinguishment of aboriginal title to vast tracts of land had been achieved through treaties with various tribes, usually negotiated under military threat. Through such treaties, Don Mitchell writes, "the United States agreed to pay money and distribute sundries to tribal members as compensation for the land the treaties ceded."[11] The land retained by Native Americans, or often the areas to which they were relocated, became "Indian reserves" (i.e., reservations), a common feature of treaties with tribes west of the Mississippi. Such land is held in trust by the government. Federal statutes and constitutional law have served to define the fiduciary duty and trust responsibility of the government to, among other things, protect Indian reservations from unwelcome third-party intrusions, although federal actions have all too often subverted that trust.

In 1871, Congress ended treaty making with Native Americans, but in Alaska the usual reasons for negotiating treaties—conflicts over land and resources that led to military actions—simply did not apply. Confrontations between whites and Natives were localized, and only a few isolated incidents involved military responses. There is little evidence that Alaska Natives impeded American business interests during the early American era. According to recent investigations by Stephen Langdon, most businessmen of that period saw no merit in picking battles with Tlingits over their ownership of salmon streams. In one example, a businessman who wanted to establish a salmon saltery in 1870 near Klawock on Prince of Wales Island paid a local clan leader a use fee. Langdon writes: "This was a clear recognition of title to the stream and the principle of lease was established to make it possible for [the] saltery to operate. A few years later in 1878, [after the sale of the saltery] the practice of lease payments to [the clan] was maintained and they continued down until at least 1897."[12]

In those decades, change was sufficiently slow that the Native people were able to gradually adapt without severe disruption to their traditional ownership rights and cultural practices, but from the mid-1890s forward the pace of change quickened. The U.S. government began to enforce ever more restrictive regulations for use and access to land and resources while American missionaries were active throughout the region, encouraging Natives, often aggressively, to abandon their old ways.[13] In 1889, Congress responded to the already-apparent overfishing in Alaska by commercial, in-stream salmon traps and passed the Alaska Salmon Fisheries Act, which banned fish weirs, traps, and other obstructions in salmon streams.[14]

At first, enforcement was inadequate, but in 1903 President Theodore Roosevelt's Alaska Salmon Commission was able to report that the practice of barricading Alaska streams had been "abolished by the salmon inspectors."[15] Prohibited by law from using in-stream methods of fishing to fulfill their subsistence needs, Natives had by then transitioned into the cash economy fostered by the commercial fishing industry. A chart presented in *Fishermen's Frontier* illustrates the level of Native and non-Native fishermen: "Indian fishermen were integral to the salmon-canning industry in southeastern Alaska, generally outnumbering white fishers in the late nineteenth and early twentieth centuries."[16]

For at least two decades (1890–1910) Native fishermen could make decent livings in the commercial fishing industry, while their families found employment in the canneries.

Fish traps, which were to dramatically alter the fisheries economy, were at first too few to pose a major threat to independent fishermen. In *Fishermen's Frontier,* David Arnold writes: "Stationary traps…required large capital investments and also had to be rebuilt yearly, as winter storms and ice floes took their toll. Such costs made trap-fishing prohibitive for most canneries."[17]

In 1907 the introduction of floating traps changed the equation. Just as Alaska Natives became fully vested in the commercial fishing industry, the relatively inexpensive and highly efficient floating fish traps began to marginalize independent fishermen who were prohibited from fishing anywhere close to the traps, which were arrayed in fixed locations along the shorelines. "The percentage of trap-caught salmon in southeastern Alaska escalated dramatically during the 1910s. Traps became the dominant form of gear."[18] Barred by law from the streams they once owned, then forced out of the most productive shoreline fishing areas,

Native fishermen found themselves fighting for scraps from a fully indus-trialized, vertically integrated fisheries industry. Native fishermen found allies among the independent white fishermen, who were similarly mar-ginalized, an alliance that would play out during the post–World War II statehood movement.

By the second decade of the twentieth century, the dispossession of Alaska Native aboriginal fishing rights, at least in Southeast, was complete.

Alaska Natives were given no more consideration with the land they occupied than the fisheries they depended upon. When the Tongass National Forest and the Glacier Bay National Monument were created by presidential proclamations, Natives' occupancy and use rights were entire-ly ignored. According to Mitchell, Congress made no effort to compen-sate Southeast Natives for appropriating the land, "even though the U.S. government's past dealings with other groups of Native Americans was precedent that it should have."[19]

The Alaska Native Brotherhood, organized in 1912, eventually took up the battle to win the compensation that had not been offered. Initially, as we shall explore in more detail, the ANB had no politically practical alternative other than to seek a large-scale cash settlement from the federal government for lost lands and rights.

Several acts of Congress in this period addressed property rights for individual Alaska Natives. The 1906 Allotment Act authorized the sec-retary of the interior to assign individual allotments of land to Alaska Natives, but the process was so onerous and the bureaucracy so disinter-ested that, according to Langdon, most Natives knew nothing about the program—and those who did found many obstacles to submitting allot-ment claims. The program may have failed to spark much interest among Natives because private land ownership did not fit with traditional con-cepts of property rights. Langdon estimates that by 1970 fewer than one hundred allotment claims had been filed in Southeast Alaska.[20]

In 1926, two years after Congress passed legislation granting citizen-ship to Native Americans, it provided, through the Alaska Native Townsite Act, a means for Alaska Natives to gain title to the land on which their habitations stood. But the title for such homes was under restricted deed, similar to the trust status of reservation land that cannot be sold, collat-eralized, or subdivided. Such deeds did not provide for a direct transfer

Tlingit seal hunters in Glacier Bay under tow by the Harriman Expedition in 1899. With the creation of Glacier Bay National Monument (1925) and its later expansion (1939), the National Park Service made no provision for Alaska Natives' customary and traditional use of the area. In the postwar years, the NPS began to treat Tlingits who were hunting and fishing in Glacier Bay as the "ecological equivalent of squatters" (Theodore Catton, Inhabited Wilderness, 31).

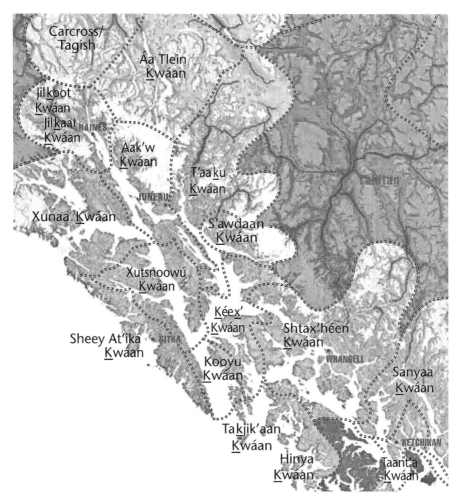

This detail of a poster developed through the research and under the guidance of the late Andy Hope illustrates the approximate boundaries of Tlingit kwaans (areas occupied by closely affiliated clans) during the mid-1800s. Map courtesy of Tlingit Readers Inc., Andrew Hope III collection.

Peter Simpson (left) and William Paul—one quiet and accommodating, the other brash and contentious—were both compelling leaders. As a team, the two men cleared the path for the ANB/ANS to initiate the Alaska Native claims movement. Photos courtesy of the Andrew Hope III collection.

of ownership, and within a few generations dozens of Alaska Native heirs would share restricted title to property that could not be sold. The benign purpose may have been to prevent sales of Native-owned homes and land to non-Native buyers, but the result was an irresolvable mess.

By the 1930s, the ANB was focused on winning compensation for lost hunting and fishing rights and for land taken to create the Tongass National Forest and Glacier Bay National Monument. ANB leaders also began, in the 1940s, a serious, prolonged debate over the merits of reservations as a means to reacquire aboriginal hunting and fishing rights and to recover large sections of traditional lands.

Soon after the Second World War, two lawsuits were filed—one (*Tlingit and Haida Indians of Alaska*) by the Tlingit-Haida Central Council (a separate organization founded and led by the ANB executive committee), the other (*Tee-Hit-Ton Indians*) by William Paul. Discussed in more detail later in this book, both lawsuits sought compensation for lost lands and resources. As it turned out, the courts refused to compensate for lost rights to resources like fish, game, and minerals and considered only the land itself and timber values, which were calculated at the time of taking (the early part of the twentieth century, when timber had low market value). Lost fishing and hunting rights were irrelevant, the courts reasoned, because all citizens had equal and open access to such common property resources. Since there had been no prior exclusive property right to fish and game, there could not have been a compensable taking.

In *Fishermen's Frontier,* Arnold presents a metaphorical comparison to illustrate the Native American perspective of open-access fisheries:

> The principle of "equal rights" to the salmon fishery was little consolation to a people whose previous system of regulating the fisheries was based on the delineation of strict property rights to fishing sites. It was as if hunter-gatherers colonized Kansas and determined that the landscape of privately owned farms would become open-access hunting grounds in which the farmers could compete equally with their invaders for game.[21]

It would not be until the ANCSA debates of the late 1960s that Congress would entertain the issue of aboriginal hunting and fishing in Alaska, now commonly referred to as "subsistence rights." And not until the passage of the Alaska National Interest Lands Conservation Act of 1980 would these rights be addressed. In the end, ANILCA provided a "subsistence preference" for all rural Alaskans, not just Natives.

The failure of the U.S. government to recognize aboriginal title and to compensate Alaska Natives for land and resources made it vulnerable to legal challenge, as became uncomfortably apparent to non-Native political leaders during the Alaska statehood movement. Although European and American powers had argued among themselves over rights of possession, no treaties had been made with Alaska Natives that might otherwise have brought some clarity and resolution to the issue of aboriginal claims.[22] The Treaty of Cession between the United States and Russia was so ambiguous that it was cited in various judicial decisions to both support and deny the existence of aboriginal title.[23] The Organic Act of 1884, which established an abbreviated form of territorial government for Alaska, sidestepped the issue of aboriginal claims by deferring to "future legislation by Congress." All subsequent acts of Congress up until the statehood era had failed to directly address the question of whether or not Alaska Natives owned the areas they used and occupied or if they held any other inherent rights.[24]

The U.S. government had an "exposed flank," to use a military metaphor. Exploiting that vulnerability, the Alaska Native Brotherhood picked up the sword and shield found in American law.

In the 1920s, ANB leaders were focused on achieving the full benefits of equal citizenship.[25] According to William Paul Sr.'s version, the thought of pressing the issue of aboriginal claims seemed to most ANB members a dangerous idea. But urged on by Alaska jurist and politician James Wickersham and goaded by the ANB's preeminent leader, Peter Simpson, they took the risk. At the 1929 ANB/ANS Grand Camp convention in Haines, the delegates resolved to file a lawsuit against the United States seeking compensation for expropriated lands and resources.

From 1929 through the statehood era, ANB leaders persisted in seeking redress for lost lands and rights. The path chosen during the 1929 Grand Camp convention was to seek compensation, which led to the parallel lawsuits *Tee-Hit-Ton* and *Tlingit and Haida Indians of Alaska*. The ANB had considered advocating the establishment of reservations since at least 1919, but the concept lacked strong support within the organization. A system of reservations for Alaska Natives was to remain an option firmly opposed by the federal bureaucracy, denounced by business interests, and viewed with skepticism and hostility in Congress. While the reservation concept elicited mixed reactions among ANB members, the leadership cleverly insisted it remain on the table as a point of negotiation.

While the *Tee-Hit-Ton* plaintiffs lost their lawsuit, the decision confirmed, indirectly, that aboriginal title existed and had not been extinguished.[26] The ruling in the second lawsuit, *Tlingit and Haida Indians*, established the validity of aboriginal title because of the the plaintiffs' "exclusive use and occupancy of that territory from time immemorial." In 1959, the court decreed that compensation was due for the property rights taken by the U.S. government, but the subsequent judgment award, announced nine years after the first decision, set recompense at only $7.5 million for the taking of 17.5 million acres—far below the recommendation of the court's own commissioner and the litigants' expectations.[27]

The two lawsuits served to demonstrate that settling aboriginal claims through the courts came with a high degree of risk, could take decades, and even if won, might garner monetary awards that would barely compensate for the effort.

The polarities of the post–World War II Alaska Native Brotherhood are illustrated in this 1946 photograph of the Wrangell Grand Camp meeting, with William Paul Sr. seated at far left and Andrew P. Hope at far right. Paul, a Republican, and Hope, a Democrat, both fought for equal rights but were far apart on matters of strategy and objectives. Photo courtesy of the Andrew Hope III collection.

The Alaska reservation option sputtered, then finally died, in the early 1950s. The only alternative routes to making good on Native claims ran through Congress or the executive branch. By the post-World War II era, the ANB's leadership had gained sufficient experience with Congress to know the odds they faced and were quite aware of the prevailing negative attitudes about Native American rights. Given the political climate during the statehood years (1945–1958), congressional action then might well have eliminated aboriginal claims in Alaska without compensation.

The administrations of Franklin Roosevelt and Harry Truman were sympathetic to Native American rights and concerns, but the political realignments that followed World War II limited the effectiveness of the executive branch, as was evident in the Truman administration's well-intended but feeble response to Alaska Native claims.

In retrospect, it is clear that even the most benign and generous congressional settlement of Alaska Native claims in the decade following World War II would have been in the millions of dollars and thousands of acres for the extinguishment of aboriginal title in Alaska rather than the nearly $1 billion and forty-four million acres conveyed in exchange for the extinguishment of all claims under the terms of ANCSA in 1971.

The legal basis for aboriginal title in Alaska is now well established, and a retrospective review of the court cases that established this title might lead one to believe that ANCSA was all but inevitable. Such 20/20 hindsight ignores the political reality that prevailed during the first half of the 1950s, when powerful national leaders believed Alaska Natives were not due any compensation at all, and even the most sympathetic did not believe that aboriginal title extended much beyond the immediate vicinity of Native villages. In the halls of Congress, the issue of Alaska Native claims stood on extremely thin ice.[28]

Throughout the postwar Alaska statehood movement, representatives of the Alaska Native Brotherhood were busy in Washington, D.C., shielding aboriginal claims from several congressional actions that would have had long-term adverse consequences for Alaska Natives. During this period, the ANB immersed itself in a series of proposals to establish reservations in Southeast Alaska while fending off attempts to eliminate the reservation option. ANB leaders were also meeting throughout the statehood era (1945–1958) as the Central Council, providing direction to the lawyers working on *Tlingit and Haida Indians v. United States* seeking recompense for lost lands and rights.[29]

There can be no accounting of all the individual Alaska Natives who helped in the fight to protect aboriginal claims, but no one person or group of loosely affiliated Alaska Natives could have exerted the influence of the ANB—an organization already in maturity by the postwar years. The ANB's effectiveness in representing Alaska Native interests at that time compares favorably to the political clout of the Alaska Federation of Natives in more recent decades.

An ANB/ANS couple, Jack and Emma Ellis, in their Yakutat home, circa late 1930s. Note the photograph of the 1929 ANB/ANS Grand Camp convention inserted in the framed portrait, upper left. Jack Ellis is identified in the key to the 1929 photo seated second from right behind the first row. (See 1929 ANB identification at the beginning of this book.) Photo courtesy of the Andrew Hope III collection.

2

The Alaska Native Brotherhood

Founded in 1912, the Alaska Native Brotherhood became the champion of equal citizenship for the Native people of Alaska. The men who organized the ANB were, on the whole, well-educated and observant Christians, most being graduates of the Presbyterian mission's Sitka Industrial and Training School (later renamed Sheldon Jackson School). By every meaningful measure, they were the equal of their white contemporaries—yet they had no rights.

At the time of the ANB's founding, Natives could not own title to property, stake mineral claims, legally operate commercial boats, or be educated in locally administered schools. Natives were not citizens, nor were they wards of the government; they could not vote in elections, but they could be sued in court; in rights, Natives were treated as foreigners, but they were punished as citizens.[30]

Sheldon Jackson and his colleagues imbued in their Native students the belief that citizenship was attainable through education, hard work, practice of the Christian faith, and the disavowal of Native culture. It was the persistent denial of citizenship, and what we now refer to as civil rights, that inspired these men, along with the women who founded the Alaska Native Sisterhood in 1915, to take action and win those rights on their own.

While the Presbyterians were a dominant influence on the ANB founders, the Russian Orthodox Church also played a formative role. In their book *Haa Kusteeyí, Our Culture: Tlingit Life Stories*, the Dauenhauers included biographies of the thirteen ANB founders,[31] noting that two of them, Paul Liberty and Eli Katanook, were active in the Orthodox church, and that Liberty had helped organize the St. Gabriel's Brotherhood, one of several such Orthodox brotherhoods that preceded the ANB.[32]

In their profile of Paul Liberty, the Dauenhauers include the recollec-
tion of Helen Howard, Liberty's daughter, about the founding of the ANB:

> Peter Simpson was the main organizer. He met with Paul
> Liberty early on, outlined the idea, and the two men talk-
> ed it over. After getting together, they invited others to
> join. They travelled around using their meager pocket
> money. Eventually they went to Juneau, where they got
> more men to join, and the ANB was officially founded.
> The idea was innovative, and it grew in various commu-
> nities.... At first, they met in homes, rotating meetings
> from house to house. They finally decided to build a hall.
> In Sitka, "Old Man Katlian" owned the land that is the
> site of the ANB Hall. He donated the land to the ANB
> through Paul Liberty, who was his Kiks.ádi clansman.[33]

The Orthodox acceptance of indigenous languages contrasted with
the attitude that prevailed among American missionaries, few of whom
spoke or attempted to learn any Tlingit; most insisted their students and
parishioners speak only English.[34] While the Russian clergy could be dis-
missive of the language and culture of the "heathens" they were attempt-
ing to convert, they were generally tolerant of—and often preached in the
first language of—their parishioners. Now, in contemporary times, the
suppression of language and culture is considered a grievous harm inflict-
ed on Native people, for which some denominations have retroactively
apologized.[35]

In the long term, the influence of the Orthodox Church faded, especially after the 1917 Bolshevik revolution ended all mission support from the
motherland.

Peter Simpson, a staunch Presbyterian, is remembered as the "father of
the ANB." He served as the first president and remained a guiding light until his death in 1947.[36] Considering Simpson's early writings, and the ANB's
charter document that called for the abandonment of old ways and made
English speaking a membership requirement, it might seem that the organization was, in its early years at least, assimilationist through and through.
For many Alaska Natives today, *assimilation* is a pejorative term. But the
ANB founders, their lives and times, present too many variations to be
pinned to the wall with a word.

In a modern context, *cultural accommodation* is a more accurate description of the social dynamic, one that embraces the disparate lifestyles and linguistic abilities of ANB members and the single most consistent aspiration of the organization: self-determination.

To all appearances, ANB leaders—dressed in suits and ties and polished shoes, with well-groomed hair and neatly trimmed moustaches—were model middle-class Americans, distinguishable only by their race. Combined with their fondness for contemporary music and dance, love of basketball, and mastery of parliamentary procedures, it is easy to be misled and to cast the first generation of ANB leaders as thoroughly assimilated. But through the research and writings of such people as Richard and Nora Dauenhauer, Sergei Kan, Stephen Langdon, the late Andy Hope, and now his son, Ishmael Hope, the nuances of the past are revealed.

As these researchers have documented, many, perhaps most, of the founders (inclusive of the dozens of men who joined during the formative years of 1912–1920) spoke fluent Tlingit or Haida, continued to participate in clan ceremonies, and married according to cultural dictates.[37]

While they were influenced by the assimilationist doctrines promoted by the Presbyterian Church, the early ANB leaders charted their own course, as they and their successors were to prove time and again. Considering the existential threat confronting Native Alaskans in those days, to question the founders' degree of cultural accommodation is to judge them by a harsh and blinkered view of the past. During the early decades of the twentieth century, Alaska Natives of Southeast faced a stark choice: adapt or perish. If census figures are accurate, a catastrophic population decline had pushed them to the edge of a demographic cliff. In 1900, Tlingits and Haidas in Alaska numbered fewer than five thousand descendants, down from the fifteen to twenty thousand people estimated at the time of first sustained contact with Euro-Americans.[38]

According to ANB historian John Hope (1923–1999), the early leaders—including Peter Simpson, Ralph Young, and Frank Price—believed that "we as a people had to move into a new society. We had not much choice in this and that to do that we had to give up our heritage, and our customs, and adopt [a] new language and a new religion, part and parcel. Learn it very thoroughly—and then compete."[39]

Modern scholars like Stephen Langdon and Ishmael Hope[40] question the degree to which early ANB leaders actually gave up their heritage. As a researcher at Sealaska Heritage Institute, Hope has listened intently to audio recordings of second- and third-generation ANB leaders recalling the founders and concludes that rather than straddling two worlds, these men and women *lived* in two worlds. "It was as if they had two world views *at the same time*, rather than one pushing out the other to make room," Hope said.[41]

In his "Alaska Storyteller" blog, Hope reflects upon his realization that in addition to using the tools of the dominant culture, ANB leaders, from the founders through subsequent generations, employed their own cultural tools: "As you look into the record, you'll find that … many of the ANB and ANS leaders were tradition bearers and *Aanyátx'i*—Noble People. Don't dismiss their traditional credentials by their mere appearance."[42]

Langdon has revealed another strategy employed by some Alaska Natives of that era to accommodate the pressures of white society: a retreat to cultural refugia. His research on Shakan, a village on northwest Prince of Wales Island, illustrates a form of adaptation selected by more traditional Tlingit. In the 1930s, Shakan was a fully functional and traditional Alaska Native community where the residents had selectively adapted by creating a modified seasonal round that incorporated new activities (trapping, gardening, commercial fishing), living in homes of hybrid construction (using elements of both traditional and modern design), working for the cannery on their terms, and using timber from the local sawmill to build and maintain a small fleet of commercial fishing vessels. They supported themselves by fusing modern with traditional, earning money through commercial fisheries and the sale of the furs collected through commercial trapping, yet they were living fully within their culture. Above all, they sought to retain ancestral cultural ties to land, language, and cultural practices by limiting the influence of the invasive culture—especially church and school—on their existence. This chosen lifestyle came to an end when U.S. marshals visited the village in the mid-1930s and threatened to remove the children unless the adults moved to a community with a school. Given the cruel choice of abandoning Shakan or losing their children, the people moved.[43]

From its beginning, the Alaska Native Brotherhood provided its members a safe haven to engage in the struggle and process of adapting to modernity. Some members consciously discarded outward traits of Native identity in their efforts to accommodate two worldviews while others continued in their roles as clan leaders, perhaps conscious of appearances to the extent that they kept their white friends in the dark about their traditional roles during ceremonial occasions.[44] Some spoke English as a first language while others were fluent only in their Native language; many were tradition bearers while others retained little if any of their indigenous languages or lifestyles. Regardless of such disparities, these men (and later the women of the Alaska Native Sisterhood) remained remarkably consistent in their resistance to any proposals or legislation that would result in them becoming wards of the government.

The life story of Rudolph Walton, a charter member of Sitka ANB Camp #1, illustrates the ambivalent circumstances faced by Native leaders early in the twentieth century. Born in 1867, Walton was one of the first graduates of the Sitka Industrial Training School. He also became one of the earliest inhabitants, along with his wife, of "The Cottages," a subdivision of the Presbyterian Sitka campus. Financed by benefactors and built by students, the individual cottages were assigned to married alumni who bought their new homes under installment plans. To acquire a cottage, Walton, as the head of household, had to sign a contract by which he promised, among other things, "to never attend heathen festivities, or to countenance heathen customs in surrounding villages."[45] This turned out to be a promise Rudolph Walton could not keep.

A charter member and elder of the First Presbyterian Church of Sitka, Walton ran afoul of the church's moral code in 1905, which led to his suspension as an elder. By then a widower, Walton had married Mary Davis, the widow of his uncle (perhaps by clan lineage), apparently in keeping with Tlingit traditions. But according to his granddaughter, Joyce Walton Shales, the issue that most scandalized his fellow elders was that he lived with Ms. Davis three days before they were married in a Christian ceremony. As Shales explains in her doctoral thesis, Rudolph Walton was negotiating

> the path between his Tlingit community and his Christian
> faith by picking and choosing which issues and events to
> become involved in according to their importance. In mar-
> rying Mary Davis according to Tlingit tradition prior to

a Presbyterian wedding, Mr. Walton indicates his respect for this particular aspect of Tlingit culture. By doing so he knew he was going to be in trouble with the Presbyterians and his calm admission of the offense and his leaving the matter up to the Church elders, left him personal dignity in the wake of this conflict.[46]

Several months before Walton's suspension, Congress had passed the Nelson Act, which legitimized discrimination in education, overriding earlier legislation specific to Alaska that provided for education in the territory without reference to race. According to Shales, "the social rules had changed" in Alaska, and "the stage was set for conflict." A key phrase in the legislation allowed for education of "white children and children of mixed blood who lead a civilized life."[47]

Despite the fact that the children of Walton's second wife, Mary Davis, were of mixed blood and had been counted, along with all children, Native and white, to establish the funding level of federal support for education, and ignoring the situation that had caused the local Native school to close, the Sitka School District refused to educate Walton's stepchildren because they were considered "uncivilized" by the standards of the day.[48]

Filed in 1906 and concluded two years later, *Davis v. Sitka School Board* was a test case supported by several old-line Presbyterians like Gov. John Brady but opposed by the new generation of Presbyterian leaders who, judging from the transcripts of their testimony against the Waltons and other plaintiffs, held Alaska Natives in contempt and defined *civilized* on the basis of race, not lifestyle.

To his supporters, Walton seemed like the ideal plaintiff to establish a definition of civilized that would be inclusive of educated Alaska Natives. He could speak, read, and write English, was a noted Tlingit artist and a tax-paying businessman with a store fronting on Sitka's main street. Tourists eagerly sought his silverwork and woodcarvings, now collector's items. By all accounts, Walton was a success story who embodied the Presbyterian aspiration for its students: that an Alaska Native Christian could indeed become civilized and worthy of citizenship. But in 1908, this rosy promise was revealed to be a cruel fiction when the judge ruled against Walton, declaring that he and his family were not civilized. As this case made all too clear, Natives were faced with the insurmountable obstacle of proving themselves civilized, which they could never overcome, not with Indian blood coursing through their veins.

Throughout his long life, Walton continued to live simultaneously in two worlds—an important leader of his clan and a businessman much admired by his open-minded white contemporaries.[49]

In 1914, the first Grand Camp convention took place in Sitka. Thirty-one men, Rudolph Walton among them, were in attendance, representing Juneau, Haines, Kake, Ketchikan, Metlakatla, Saxman, Sitka, and Wrangell. By the 1920s, Alaska Native communities throughout Southeast Alaska had established local camps. While the ANB styled itself as an Alaska-wide organization and encouraged the establishment of "camps" throughout the territory, no permanent camps took root outside of Southeast until decades after statehood. All of the men who have served as ANB Grand Camp presidents were Tlingit, Haida, or Tsimshian.

With member dues, coupled with the fundraising efforts of the Alaska Native Sisterhood, the ANB acquired the financial strength to support political candidates and to fund lobbying efforts in the territorial capital of Juneau and in Washington, D.C.

Although initial members of the Alaska Native Brotherhood were all churchgoers who adhered to strong Christian principles, the ANB—all Native and secular—stood apart from other Native religious brotherhoods common in this era, most of which were dominated by non-Native pastors or priests. The ANB's independence from white religious leaders, who could be as controlling as they were condescending,[50] no doubt added to the organization's credibility with other Alaska Natives—especially those who had no intention of learning English or setting aside their culture.

The primary issues in those days included voting privileges, public access for Alaska Natives (i.e., civil rights), education, health, and the abolition of fish traps.

In the 1920s, as the membership expanded and as citizenship and voting rights were achieved, the ANB relaxed its stance on rejection of Native traditions and language. In the face of the political reality that most of the village leadership spoke little English, the rule that limited membership only to English speakers was quietly dropped.

It was during the 1920s that the Paul brothers, William and Louis, rose to prominence through their association with the Alaska Native Brotherhood. They are generally recognized as among the most important of the second generation of ANB leaders. "I really don't know what we would have done without them," said Judson Brown (1912–1998), a leader from the Haines area. Brown became a member of the ANB in the 1920s and, as a teenager, attended the historic 1929 Grand Camp convention in Haines.[51]

Louis and William were the sons of Louis and Tillie Paul, both Tlingit through their mothers—Louis's father was French while Tillie's was Scottish. Tillie's husband, Louis, disappeared in December 1886 during a canoe trip, leaving the young mother caring for two boys: three-year-old Samuel and one-year-old William. She was also pregnant with the son she would name after her late husband. At the invitation of Sheldon Jackson, the widow moved her family to Sitka, where she was employed at the Sitka Industrial and Training School, working herself up from laundress to matron and resident musician. During this time, she married William Tamaree. Tillie earned her place in history when, in 1922, she violated voting laws, was arrested, went to trial, and was successfully defended by her son William, by that time an attorney. There can be little doubt that many of William Paul's strongest characteristics—intelligence, stubbornness, certitude, and determination—owed much to his mother.[52]

When he was fourteen, William was sent to Gen. Richard Pratt's Carlisle Indian School in Pennsylvania, where, according to Haycox, he was exposed to the teachings of Pratt, who "believed militantly in acculturation and assimilation as the only viable alternative to the extermination of Native Americans."[53]

William later graduated from Whitworth College, a Presbyterian school located at the time in Tacoma, Washington. He attended San Francisco Theological Seminary for one year, and then took a correspondence course in law from LaSalle University of Philadelphia. Among his many firsts, Paul became the first Alaska Native to pass the Alaska bar (1921) and the first Native elected to the Alaska Territorial Legislature (1924).

At the urging of his brother Louis, then serving as Grand Camp president of the ANB, William attended the 1920 Grand Camp convention in Wrangell, where he was elected grand secretary. Thus commenced William

Paul's turbulent, productive, and controversial association with the Alaska Native Brotherhood, lasting until his death in 1976 at the age of ninety-one.

The Paul brothers, as Haycox has written, believed that Indians were U.S. citizens by virtue of the Fourteenth Amendment and, as such, were free to control their own destiny. The two helped politicize the ANB and focus its leadership on achieving "equality, autonomy, and self-direction." When the ANB sent William Paul to Washington, D.C., in 1921, Haycox states that his testimony against fish traps "gave form and credibility" to the organization. A year later, William Paul put into play the "Indian vote" he had organized in Southeast Alaska, reasoning that "if the ANB could use political power on behalf of Indians and their rights and concerns, control of a reliable bloc of voters also would make him personally and politically powerful."[54] Paul directed the voters he influenced to support "Wickite" candidates (followers of Judge James Wickersham, who had served several terms as Alaska's delegate to Congress) in return for their support on a variety of issues of importance to him and the ANB. According to Haycox, in several close Southeast elections in 1922, "[Paul's] bloc of Indian voters was decisive."[55]

The issue for which William Paul would eventually call in his political favors involved land and resources lost by Alaska Natives because the U.S. government did not recognize aboriginal rights in Alaska.

In his book *Then Fight For It*, Fred Paul, William's son, writes that the land issue came to a head in 1921 when George Dalton and his family, Tlingits from Hoonah, were run off their potato patch on an island in Icy Strait by a rifle-wielding white man who claimed his rights to the island by virtue of a federal fox farm permit. This was but one of many similar incidents that outraged Alaska Natives.[56]

The land ownership issue came down to who was entitled to occupy areas long used by Alaska Natives for subsistence purposes. The U.S. government, without regard for any prior claims by the Native people, issued use permits for fox farms, recognized mining claims, and granted land title to cannery owners and others. According to William Paul, there were those in the ANB's membership who questioned the wisdom of making a fight over "Indian title," fearing that to do so would jeopardize the organization's top priority, the attainment of first-class citizenship. If Natives were truly equal, they reasoned, how could they ask for special rights? But

The Alaska Native Brotherhood Camp #1 meeting in Sitka in the early 1930s. Photo courtesy of the Andrew Hope III collection.

the old man himself, Peter Simpson, was not put off by such fears. In the mid-1920s, he famously whispered in the ear of William Paul Sr., asking rhetorically, "Is the land yours, Willie?" Paul answered in the affirmative and heard in reply, "Then fight for it!"[57]

Apparently, this was typical of Simpson. "He wasn't the kind of orator who was a forceful speaker," John Hope recalled. "He was very sincere; he spoke very gently and with a lot of wisdom. And he was responsible for many of the things that were accomplished by other leaders because he was behind the scenes leading things along."[58]

At the 1929 Grand Camp Convention in Haines, Grand Camp President William Paul Sr. introduced his friend and mentor, Judge James Wickersham (1857–1939), whose last term as Alaska's nonvoting delegate to Congress had ended in 1921. Wickersham was again seeking election as delegate, this time to succeed his protégé, Dan Sutherland.

"After listening to the Hon. James Wickersham give a lecture on the relation of the Tlingit and Haida Indians to dispossessed lands without compensation, the convention appointed a committee to investigate and report its findings [on bringing suit against the government]," John Hope recalled in his unpublished manuscript history of the ANB.

The Grand Camp accepted the committee's report, and thus was born the Alaska Native claims movement.[59]

Judson Brown, who witnessed the speech at the 1929 convention, recalled that Wickersham, "as early as 1912, had gone up to consult with the Athabascans and with several Eskimo groups, and had tried to urge them to organize so that they could bring suit against the government for lands that they had lost. In each attempt, Judge Wickersham had been unsuccessful."[60]

According to Wickersham's diary entries,[61] he had consulted with the Athabascans of the Tanana region in July 1915 about establishing reservations to protect fishing and hunting rights, though the assembled chiefs chose not to petition the government for such protection. As Brown remembered, ANB members were aware that if they followed Wickersham's advice they would be the first Alaska Natives to sue the United States.

With the Convention's acceptance of the committee report, Wickersham's recommendations were put into effect. "We began actively seeking out lawyers and solutions and bending the arms of several legislators,

ALASKA NATIVE SISTERHOOD - 1930 CONVENTION - KETCHIKAN, ALASKA

The ANS at the 1930 Grand Camp convention in Ketchikan. While the women of the ANS were often praised for their fundraising prowess, they were also contributing to the discourse and decision-making process. "We [the ANB and ANS] always had meetings together and we listened to each other.... Of course [when] the women said anything, it went. No opposition. Traditionally, the women were the treasurers" (Reverend Dr. Walter Soboleff, In Sisterhood, 43). Photo courtesy of the Andrew Hope III collection.

In 1921, the ANB sent William Paul to Washington, D.C., where he testified before Congress in opposition to industrial fish traps of the type pictured above. The traps, highly efficient and relatively cheap to operate, drove down salmon prices along with the income of fishermen, Native and non-Native alike. Paul's testimony put the ANB on the map as a political force to be reckoned with. Photo courtesy of the Alaska Historical Library.

principally the delegates from Alaska, toward getting the legislation that we would need to actually permit us to sue the United States government," Brown said.[62]

As Wickersham had explained to Grand Camp delegates, Congress had to pass a jurisdictional act to grant the Tlingit and Haida people standing in court so they could seek compensation from the federal government for any outstanding claims.

During his prior service as Alaska's nonvoting delegate to Congress—the only territory-wide elected position in Alaska—Wickersham had witnessed several jurisdictional acts pass Congress, granting certain Native American tribes the right to sue the federal government in the U.S. Court of Claims to receive compensation for the expropriation of traditional lands and resources. Beginning his campaign for another term as Alaska's congressional delegate when he spoke to the Grand Camp convention, Wickersham promised to introduce a jurisdictional act for Southeast Alaska Natives should he be elected.[63]

Wickersham won reelection, and in December 1931 he fulfilled his promise by persuading U.S. Senator Lynn Frazier (R-ND) to introduce a jurisdictional act to give the Native people of Southeast Alaska standing in the U.S. Court of Claims. As Don Mitchell explains, the bill failed after meeting with resistance from the President Hoover's Commissioner of Indian Affairs Charles Rhoads, who "opposed the measure…because there was no precedent for paying a group of Native Americans compensation for the extinguishment of aboriginal title that had not been recognized by a treaty."[64]

Rhoades's objection underscored what was to become a core issue: does aboriginal title exist if not recognized by treaty? According to Haycox, a landmark opinion by Nathan Margold, the Department of Interior's solicitor (legal adviser) in the mid-1930s, held that a treaty was not necessary because "Indian tribes retained all their original powers, their internal sovereignty, unless such had been formally extinguished by the Congress."[65]

Langdon and others credit Felix Cohen (Margold's subordinate) for articulating the concept that aboriginal rights preexisted European colonization. In other words, a treaty was not necessary to recognize that which already existed. But until the lawsuits promoted by the ANB and William Paul were heard in federal court in the 1950s, the preexisting rights of Alaska Natives had little currency. The presumption of unrestricted federal entitlement to Alaska remained fiercely defended by business interests, most white politicians, and the bureaucrats of government agencies.

Changes at the top of the federal bureaucracy followed Franklin D. Roosevelt's election as president in 1932. Shortly after his inauguration, President Roosevelt appointed Harold Ickes, a progressive Republican, as secretary of the interior, under whom Felix Cohen was to serve as a solicitor. At Ickes's urging, Roosevelt also appointed John Collier as commissioner of Indian affairs. Collier, who was known for his opposition to the forced assimilation of Native Americans, became a leading advocate of Native American self-determination and a principal advocate for change and reform in his department.

In Alaska, the only national candidates the territory's citizens could vote for were those competing for the seat of nonvoting delegate to Congress. In the 1932 election, Democrat Anthony "Tony" Dimond, a former Alaska prospector turned attorney, challenged the Republican incumbent, James Wickersham.

Dimond, who was of a new generation, campaigned by airplane and on radio, while Wickersham favored steamship and rail travel and eschewed radio. But the two candidates shared an open-minded attitude towards Alaska Natives that was atypical of the era. Dimond won his seat in Congress along with Democrats across the county who were swept into office by an electorate motivated to vote for change in the midst of the Great Depression.[66]

According to historian Robert Price, Dimond worked closely with the ANB and was a reliable supporter of Alaska Native interests during his twelve years as Alaska's nonvoting delegate.[67]

William Paul, who was to continue his affiliation with the Republican Party throughout his life, was nonpartisan in his associations with those who could advance his causes. He and Dimond developed a close working relationship during Roosevelt's first four-year term, a crucial period in the modern history of Native Americans.

Then at the height of his influence inside the ANB, Paul had by this time made his mark as a relentless advocate of Alaska Native rights and progressive issues, largely through his Ketchikan-based monthly, the *Alaska Fisherman* (1923–1932), an outlet for his opinions on the issues of the day and an effective means of advancing his political objectives. Like James Wickersham and Harold Ickes, Paul was of the progressive wing of the Republican Party and championed such issues as wage equity, the right to unionize, and equal rights.[68]

Paul's first experience lobbying Congress came in 1921, when he was sent by the ANB to Washington, D.C., to testify in opposition to fish traps.[69] By 1934, when Congress took under consideration the Jurisdictional Act and, on a much larger scale, enacted legislation to reform the Indian policy of the United States, Paul was a recognized leader of the ANB. Dimond described him as "an attorney at law, [who] has served as a member of the Alaskan Legislature and is a very able man. He is now a member of the [ANB] executive committee."[70]

Dimond rewrote the jurisdictional act first drafted by Judge Wickersham and had it introduced in Congress. After some amendments requested by the Department of the Interior, Congress passed the Jurisdictional Act of 1935, which enabled the Tlingit and Haida people to pursue "all claims of whatever nature, legal or equitable, [that they] may have against the United States" in the U.S. Court of Claims.[71] If it could be proved in court that the Native people of Southeast Alaska had held aboriginal title to the land and resources taken for the creation of the Tongass National Forest and Glacier Bay National Monument, the United States would be obligated to pay compensation. While the court could validate a claim and establish the compensation due, it could not grant title to land or order access to the resources.

Considering that the federal government had made it illegal for Alaska Natives to fish by traditional methods in the salmon streams from which they had harvested the majority of their sustenance, the litigants believed this loss of fishing prerogatives deserved as much or more compensation than for the lands that had been taken.[72] A subtext to their grievances about lost fishing rights was the topic of fish traps. Owned by cannery interests, the traps were the principal reason Native fisherman had become increasingly marginalized and impoverished. Alaska Natives, especially along the coastal areas, had good reason to feel double-crossed by the government. Trap robbing became widespread, often rationalized as stealing from the rich to support the poor.

This jurisdictional act held relevance only for the Native people of Southeast Alaska. Of much greater national importance was the Indian Reorganization Act (IRA) of 1934—the "New Deal for Native Americans"—which would overhaul U.S. Indian policy. John Collier is recognized for his role as a leading proponent of this legislation.

The men who served as Alaska's congressional delegate, especially Wickersham and Sutherland, had come to depend on the ANB as the go-to organization on all matters of concern to Alaska Natives, and for this reason, the newly elected Dimond consulted the ANB on the legislation to reform U.S. Indian policy.[73]

Responding to the ANB's recommendations, Dimond attempted to modify the language of the IRA "to insert references to Alaska Natives at appropriate locations in the text to enable Natives to obtain the educational and other benefits the bill made available, including the right to organize the same business corporations that tribes whose members resided on reservations were authorized to organize."[74]

Andy Hope in 1984, while serving as executive director of the Sitka Community Association (later known as the Sitka Tribe of Alaska), discusses budget issues with Mark Jacobs Jr. (center) and Al Perkins (right), both SCA Council members. Ted Wright is in the foreground. Under Hope's leadership, this organization was at the forefront of the Alaska tribal movement. Like many other Alaska IRAs, SCA was organized soon after the Indian Reorganization Act was amended in 1936. Photo by Peter Metcalfe.

The Alaska references, for the most part, failed to survive the conference committee, of which Dimond was not a member. As a consequence of the legislation's focus on Indian tribes and reservations, Alaska issues were not addressed in the 1934 legislation.

In 1935, William Paul Sr. was in Washington, D.C., working on the Jurisdictional Act when he took the opportunity to discuss amending the IRA with sympathetic officials at the highest levels of the Department of the Interior—including John Collier, commissioner of Indian affairs, and interior solicitor Felix Cohen—to extend its provisions to Alaska. The effort met with success. According to Mitchell, while drafting amendments to the IRA, Collier and Cohen also "decided to grant the secretary of the interior new authority to protect Native land use and fish and game harvest opportunities."[75] The provision that granted the authority, Section

2, allowed the secretary of the interior to establish reservations in Alaska without congressional consent.

Paul, who was philosophically opposed to reservations, urged Dimond to lobby the bill's drafters to make the IRA's economic provisions broadly applicable to Alaska, which required a substitution for language referencing tribes and reservations. As Robert Price observes in *The Great Father in Alaska,* "the version of Felix Cohen's bill that Dimond introduced in January 1936 contained a proviso that authorized 'Indian-chartered corporations in Alaska' to be organized 'without regard to residence on any Indian reservation.'" In other words, Alaska Natives would not have to be members of federally recognized tribes to enjoy the benefits of the so-called New Deal for Native Americans.

The amended IRA allowed Alaska villages to create organizations that could apply for federal loans. Constitutions had to be written and, when approved by the Department of the Interior, tribal governments came into being. In the case of Alaska IRAs, none had a land base, which put them outside the realm of "Indian Country," with ramifications that continue to adversely affect Alaska Native sovereignty. While the resulting entities (e.g., Sitka Community Association, Organized Village of Kake, the Hydaburg Cooperative Association) were closer in concept to savings-and-loan institutions than to conventional tribes, the Alaska IRAs were de facto tribal entities and, in 1994, became federally recognized tribes.[76]

The lawsuit permitted by the Jurisdictional Act, *Tlingit and Haida Indians of Alaska v. United States,* would absorb the attention of the ANB membership for more than three decades (1935–1968). The act required the secretary of the interior to approve attorney contracts, which Paul and other ANB leaders apparently expected to be a mere formality. The effort to initiate a lawsuit got off to a rocky start when the Alaska Office of Indian Affairs (OIA—renamed the Bureau of Indian Affairs in 1947) insisted on a role in the process. The Alaska OIA used the provision requiring the secretary's approval to assert control over attorney selection, offending the ANB's leadership and most especially William Paul, a focus of OIA invective. As Haycox observes, "In the lower forty-eight states, most Indian groups were poorly organized....In Alaska, however, the Tlingit and Haida people were well organized politically, and operated quite independently of federal advice and control."[77] The ANB had no issue with accepting financial help from the OIA, but they were not about to be told what to do, how to do it, or whom to hire to act on their behalf.

The tension between the Alaska Office of Indian Affairs and the ANB took the lawsuit down a tortuous path. William Paul opted to ignore the OIA, which not only delayed the legal process but also worked to his personal disadvantage when other events overtook him. In 1937, Paul was disbarred over a charge that he had embezzled from clients of his law practice. Exactly what happened is clouded by the politics and prejudices of the era. By this time, Paul had come to be despised by the cannery and mining interests that depended to one degree or another on Native labor and felt threatened by the Native voting bloc that Paul had organized. He was also much disliked and distrusted by what had become the anti-Paul faction of the ANB leadership, which coalesced around the Peratrovich brothers—Frank and Roy—from the Klawock area. In any event, Paul chose not to defend himself in the disbarment proceedings.

Don Mitchell, who takes a jaundiced view of William Paul in *Sold American*, nonetheless gives him due credit: "during [Paul's] first years of prominence his work on behalf of the ANB was as courageous as it was important, since many whites considered Paul a dangerous and impudent Indian."[78]

In the eyes of his antagonists, the disbarment brought shame upon Paul and, to a certain degree, upon the ANB, but for the rest of his life Paul retained the loyalty of a substantial percentage of the ANB membership, support that ebbed and flowed at the margin of a majority.[79]

After his disbarment, Paul was fighting a rearguard action, pinning his hopes and plans on his sons, William Jr. (hereinafter "Bill Paul Jr.") and Fred, both of whom received their law degrees in 1939. The younger Pauls quickly engaged in legal work on behalf of their father and their uncle, Louis, as well as the ANB. That same year, William Paul Sr. was back in action, once again "in control of the ANB, so much so that when the 1939 Grand Camp convened at Sitka in November, the delegates elected Louis Paul to a fourth term as grand president and elected Bill Paul to succeed his father as grand secretary."[80]

Office of Indian Affairs officials viewed with dismay the resurgence of the Paul faction within the Alaska Native Brotherhood. As William Paul began to choreograph a series of actions by the ANB so he, and the

His white antagonists considered William Paul "a dangerous and impudent Indian," according to author Don Mitchell. William Paul is pictured here, circa 1906, at Whitworth College, where he was the starting quarterback on the football team. While he is likely posing for the camera, Paul's demeanor reflects the dogged determination for which he would become well known. Photo courtesy of Whitworth University Archives.

ANB, could take charge of the litigation, the tone of the correspondence between Paul and the agency deteriorated, marked by Paul's obdurate opinions and the agency's barely contained intolerance of an Indian who refused to be controlled.

If the federal officials imagined that other ANB leaders would be easier to deal with, they were right. The people who would succeed William Paul and his supporters were, on the whole, more deferential and not nearly so abrasive. But that was as far as it went. The ANB leadership remained united in their determination to supervise the lawsuit and chart their own course. The bureaucratic obstructions to the Tlingit and Haida lawsuit continued unabated.

Kookwasx (left) at her fish camp (circa 1900) located near the present-day site of the Juneau airport. Both the Tee-Hit-Ton and Tlingit and Haida lawsuits sought compensation for lost lands and resources, but the federal courts ignored Native use of fish and game, which were deemed to be subject to common property rights. The Tee-Hit-Ton claim was rejected by the U.S. Supreme Court while the U.S. Court of Claims found in favor of Tlingit and Haida but rejected any compensation for the fishery property claim, the main economic loss suffered by the Tlingit and Haida people. Photo courtesy of Ike Cropley, grandson of Kookwasx.

3

Suing the Government

In mid-November 1935, the ANB organized the first official meeting of the Tlingit and Haida Indians in Wrangell, Alaska, for the purpose of taking "such action as might be deemed necessary to accept the terms of said [Jurisdictional Act]." Each Native community in Southeast Alaska had elected several delegates to send to the mass meeting in Wrangell; there, one delegate from each community was elected to the Central Council. The Central Council then appointed William Paul as attorney to prosecute the suit against the United States and advised him to select an associate whose name would be submitted to the Central Council. Paul promptly informed the meeting he would ask Judge James Wickersham to associate himself in the case.[81]

This initial organizing effort by the ANB proved futile, as the Office of Indian Affairs insisted that only a tribal entity (as defined by the OIA), not a dues-paying membership organization like the ANB, could file a lawsuit under the terms of the Jurisdictional Act.

The effort was also hobbled by the difficulty of raising funds in the middle of the Great Depression, the eventual withdrawal of the aging Wickersham, and William Paul's distracting plan to organize the ANB as a region-wide corporation under the terms of the Indian Reorganization Act as amended in 1936. Paul's disbarment further complicated this initial organizing phase.

William Paul did not stay down for long. At the 1939 Grand Camp convention in Sitka, he orchestrated the introduction and acceptance of Resolution 37, which authorized the executive committee of the Alaska Native Brotherhood to serve as the Tlingit-Haida Central Council. By this means, the ANB proposed to conform itself to provisions of the Jurisdictional Act of 1935. Oscar Chapman, assistant secretary of the interior, objected. Addressing a letter to William Paul Sr., Chapman proposed that his department would instead recognize the Indian Reorganization Act councils (IRAs) that had been established in several Southeast Native communities as de facto tribes.[82] None of this had much effect—the Central Council and its lawsuit remained under the control of the ANB (acting as the Central Council), although not without continued objections from the OIA.

The ANB at least made the appearance of conforming to the dictates of Indian Affairs bureaucrats. In an interview with Andy Hope, Judson Brown recalled that sequential meetings were held. "We had the ANB Convention going on at the ANB Hall and we were able to get space at the Salvation Army Hall to hold our Tlingit-Haida meetings.... That was when we first fulfilled the requirements of organizing."[83] Federal officials thought otherwise, viewing the ANB's effort to create a mirror organization (the Tlingit-Haida Claims Committee, a.k.a. the Tlingit-Haida Central Council) as a provocation for ignoring their insistence that only attorneys approved by the department and supervised by the Office of Indian Affairs could prosecute Indian claims.[84] According to Haycox, Alaska Native leaders viewed these as poor excuses, believing that the OIA officials "simply did not take easily to Natives controlling their own destinies."[85]

In addition to the condescension that pervaded the bureaucracy, at the root of this battle between the ANB and the Department of the Interior (Indian Affairs) was the contempt many senior officials held for William Paul. For this and many other reasons, Paul's opponents in the ANB began to get the upper hand. In 1940, Andrew P. Hope (1896–1968), a longtime ANB activist and former Grand Camp president, was elected to lead the newly organized Central Council. Progress was further delayed by the interruption of World War II. Finally, in 1946, James E. Curry (1907–1972), a Chicago attorney who was working as general counsel for the newly formed National Congress of American Indians, was accepted by both the Central Council and the Department of the Interior at the recommendation of Felix Cohen,[86] one of the architects of the Indian Reorganization Act. Curry succeeded in filing the lawsuit with the U.S. Court of Claims in 1947, but then found his efforts to pass the case on to other attorneys—

Andrew P. Hope, the founding president of the Central Council of Tlingit and Haida Indians, and his son, John Hope, who would later lead the Central Council as its CEO and president, at a Grand Camp convention in the 1960s. Photo courtesy of the Andrew Hope III collection.

Israel "Lefty" Weissbrodt and David Cobb—stymied by the department.[87] Weissbrodt and Cobb, after overcoming the initial bureaucratic obstacle, and many other impediments and delays, finally succeeded in arguing the lawsuit before the U.S. Court of Claims in 1957.

But William Paul had gotten there first. With the help of attorney J.C. Peacock of Washington, D.C., and his sons Bill Jr. and Fred, Paul's lawsuit *Tee-Hit-Ton Indians v. United States* was filed on October 30, 1951, in the U.S. Court of Claims. While Paul Sr.'s motivation for breaking away from the Central Council's lawsuit, of which he was the progenitor, is too fraught a topic to discuss in detail here, it should be noted that the legal claims in *Tee-Hit-Ton* were rooted in a solid ethnographic principle: for Tlingits, property ownership resided with the clan.[88] (In modern orthography, the name of Paul's clan is spelled "Teeyhittaan," one of more than a dozen clans of the Raven moiety.)

William Paul, his sons, and Peacock based their case on the reasoning that Alaska Natives were citizens, not wards of the government as they would have been as members of the type of tribal entity the Office of Indian Affairs preferred to recognize. Instead, the Pauls presented the theory that since Alaska Natives had never been "tribal members," they were like any other citizens, and, as provided for in the U.S. Constitution, the property of citizens could not be taken without due process and fair compensation.[89] While the Pauls did not put it in these terms, their case presented clans as similar to modern corporations, which have every right to sue the U.S. government on behalf of corporate shareholders for uncompensated taking of property. Since clan-owned property had been taken by the federal government without due process or any compensation, if *Tee-Hit-Ton* prevailed, the clans, not the collective Tlingit and Haida people, would have received cash compensation. Considering the uncertainties of clan membership, a scheme to distribute a cash award would likely have defied a fair and practical solution.[90]

Although it's interesting to speculate on what might have happened, the federal judiciary shut the door on William Paul's theory. In April of 1954, the Court of Claims issued its decision, ruling that because neither the 1867 Treaty of Cession nor the 1884 Organic Act, nor any other federal statute had recognized Alaska Native aboriginal title, the plaintiffs were not entitled to compensation for land and resources taken over the years. The decision, affirmed by the U.S. Supreme Court a year later, found that Congress had yet to address the question of aboriginal title in Alaska.[91]

As historian Stephen Haycox writes, the court's language opened a world of opportunity: "[When] the Court said Congress had not recognized the Tee-Hit-Ton title, it implied that the title had been there either for Congress to recognize or not. It was the first judicial confirmation of aboriginal title in Alaska, and it would apply to all Native groups across the territory."[92]

While the decision represented a huge loss for William Paul and his sons, it proved to be a victory for Alaska Native claims: the highest court in the land had implicitly recognized that aboriginal title actually existed in Alaska.

The lawsuit filed ahead of *Tee-Hit-Ton—Tlingit and Haida Indians v. United States*[93]—dragged on through the 1950s.

Most of the ANB leadership, the organization's rank and file, and the Native population of Southeast in general began to lose faith that anything good would come of the *Tlingit and Haida* lawsuit. Andrew P. Hope, his supporters, and the attorneys who succeeded Curry nevertheless persevered. In the face of numerous setbacks and procedural obstacles, Lefty Weissbrodt and David Cobb succeeded in arguing the case in 1957 before the U.S. Court of Claims, which found in 1959 that Southeast Alaska Natives did indeed have as yet uncompensated claims, the aboriginal title to which had been extinguished by extralegal action of the U.S. government in creating, by presidential orders, the Tongass National Forest and Glacier Bay National Monument. Not many dots had to be connected to realize that the court's decision cast a dark cloud over title to vast portions of Alaska.

The *Tlingit and Haida* judgment award process, by which the compensation would be determined, took another nine years, a period in which the Central Council grappled with an issue that had bedeviled the organization since its inception: Who would get the money?

Haycox explains how the matter was resolved:

> In 1965, Tlingit-Haida Central Council requested the U.S. Congress to remedy this difficulty by making the award to a new organization, now officially named the Central Council of Tlingit and Haida Indians Tribes of Alaska (CCTHITA), and recognizing it as the proper recipient of the expected award rather than to the eighteen separate Southeast communities.... [Congress agreed] and directed CCTHITA to elect members, prepare a roll of all Tlingit and Haida people living and to make plans for use of the settlement.[94]

Even after the 1959 decision by the Court of Claims, most politicians persisted in discounting the significance of aboriginal title. Alaska's first elected governor, Bill Egan, presided over an administration that went ahead with land selections with little if any regard to Native interests. But others—in particular those who were trying to launch Alaska's oil industry—began to ponder the longer-term economic implications. Since

aboriginal title actually existed, it would have to be extinguished throughout much of Alaska before serious oil development could begin.

As Haycox explains, experiences in litigating *Tlingit and Haida* contributed to the success of the drive for a comprehensive settlement of Alaska
Native claims:

> Experience gained in working with the Indian Office
> and the Department of the Interior was passed from one
> generation to another, and from Tlingit-Haida leaders to
> other regional Native leaders, both before and after the
> formation of the Alaska Federation of Natives in 1966.
> The internecine battles within the ANB and its succes-
> sor organizations helped to clarify the issues involved in
> aboriginal claims, and made plain the need for unity. The
> various suits undertaken by William Paul Sr. further clar-
> ified the issues, and showed the futility of relying on the
> courts for a clear confirmation of claims.[95]

While the 1959 *Tlingit and Haida* decision established a sound legal
basis for aboriginal claims, the subsequent judgment award, released nine
years later, was only $7.5 million for the taking of 17.5 million acres (about
forty-three cents per acre). The amount was based, as Haycox points out,
"on the commercial value of accessible timber in 1905, the date of the taking [by the creation of the Tongass National Forest]."[96] As the dissenting
judge, Philip Nichols Jr., observed, the judgment failed to even consider
the substantial indirect costs associated with the loss of fishing rights. The
$7.5 million award was a stunning disappointment to most *Tlingit and
Haida* plaintiffs.

Ill with the cancer that would soon end his life, Andrew Hope Sr.
looked at the settlement philosophically and replied to those who be-
moaned the judgment award: "In the greatest country on earth, in the
highest court of the land, we won our case."[97]

Carrying forward in Hope's spirit, a new generation of leaders, with
John Borbridge Jr. as Central Council president, invested the judgment
award, which became the foundation upon which the modern organization was built. The Central Council of Tlingit and Haida Indian Tribes,
no longer operating under the wing of the Alaska Native Brotherhood, was
now a full-fledged organization with its own offices, staff, and financial

resources. The Central Council, Haycox explains, brought expertise and more to the table:

> By 1971... [the Central Council] had been for some time in a position to make all of its valuable resources and experience available to the [Alaska Federation of Natives]. Indeed, in that year, the [Central Council] made a loan of $100,000 to the AFN for the final months of the drive toward the settlement act.[98]

In addition to the Central Council's $100,000 loan, a substantial sum in those days, the AFN's campaign for statewide settlement benefited from the addition of John Borbridge to the team. Bill Van Ness, who served as special counsel to the U.S. Senate Energy and Natural Resources Committee under Senator Henry "Scoop" Jackson (D-WA), during the lobbying effort to settle Alaska Native claims, affirmed the importance of Borbridge's contributions: "I remember one time when it looked like we wouldn't get the [ANCSA] legislation, and John [Borbridge] spoke without notes for 40 minutes, an amazing delivery, better than many constitutional lawyers I've seen. He had a lot of impact, especially with the Republicans because he spoke to legalities, to the constitutional issues. His argument was well reasoned, there was no banging on the table."[99]

Considering all, it would appear that the capitalization of the Central Council had a considerable influence on ANCSA's treatment of Southeast Alaska. In this light, the acceptance of the $7.5 million award can be seen as one of the wisest financial decisions ever made by a group of Native Americans. The amount of equity value that was to be acquired by Sealaska, the regional corporation, and the two urban and ten village corporations of Southeast Alaska, and the subsequent cash distributions by these Native corporations in the years since ANCSA became law in 1971, all but defies calculation.[100]

The Central Council might have rejected the award, continued the litigation, and taken another path, but speculation of this nature assumes better alternatives that were almost surely unobtainable during the years ANCSA was under consideration.

Following the settlement of Alaska Native claims, the Central Council's executive committee became the interim board of directors for the nascent Sealaska Corporation. Today, the Central Council of Tlingit

The flag raising at the Mt. Edgecumbe Hospital in 1986 signified the transfer of authority for health and medical care from the Indian Health Service to the Native-owned Southeast Alaska Regional Health Consortium (SEARHC), an organization founded by the ANB/ANS. SEARHC is now the largest health care organization in Southeast Alaska. Photo by Peter Metcalfe.

and Haida Indian Tribes of Alaska stands as an autonomous, federally recognized tribe that has taken charge of most functions previously performed by the Bureau of Indian Affairs. Sealaska and the twelve urban/village corporations of Southeast Alaska now have collective enrollments exceeding twenty-two thousand Alaska Native shareholders and currently hold title to nearly six hundred thousand acres of an eventual entitlement that will total 648,400 acres.[101]

None of this is to say that ANCSA fulfilled the aspirations of Alaska Natives. It is far too flawed a settlement. For many Alaska Natives, the most glaring flaw of all is that it effectively disinherited all Alaska Natives born after the legislation was signed into law. But when considering the pros and cons of ANCSA, one should not lose sight of the nonmonetary benefits for all Alaska Natives, such as political influence, cultural pride, and self-determination, all of which have strengthened and flourished in the decades since 1971.

One of the points made in the following chapters is that in ANCSA, the Alaska Native Brotherhood attained its bottom-line objectives: compensation for land and resources lost, control over land and resources recovered, and the freedom to make decisions without government control.

Father Duncan in his study at Metlakatla. An English-born Anglican missionary to Canada, Duncan broke away from his church and led a group of Tsimshians from British Columbia to "New Metlakatla" on Annette Island, which later became a federally recognized reservation, the only one of its type now operating in Alaska. Duncan remains a controversial figure: a domineering prelate who insisted his Native parishioners learn English, abandon traditional practices, adopt Protestant values, and follow his guidance. Nonetheless, his reservation became a model of communal industriousness and stood as an exception to the rule: most reservations in the States were sinks of poverty. Photo courtesy of the Alaska Historical Library.

4

Reservations in Alaska

ANB leaders had long been aware that reservations were an option, but from the beginning most were philosophically opposed to the idea. In the November 1919 issue of the *Verstovian*, Louis Paul, writing about the proceedings of a recent Grand Camp convention, recounted that Peter Simpson spoke against reservations because "American ideals develop best where American ideals exist and these are not found best on reservations." Louis recounted his own remarks against reservations as "not conducive to proper advancement because of racial segregation. Such segregation does not give proper environment [and] is un-American in principle by setting apart the Indian American for special legislation."[102]

In Southeast Alaska, reservations for Klawock and Hydaburg had been established early in the twentieth century, but were withdrawn by executive order after village residents protested. As Wickersham learned in 1915 when he consulted with the Athabascan chiefs of the Tanana region, opposition to reservations was widespread, mostly fueled by resistance to becoming wards of the federal government. While there were other reasons Alaska Natives opposed reservations, none should be interpreted as an acceptance of the status quo. Natives throughout Alaska were keenly aware that they had once owned the land and resources that had been taken, and they persisted in voicing their grievances and seeking just compensation or the return of property rights.

Twenty years after the meeting recorded in the *Verstovian*, ANB members began to take another look. The motivation was twofold. First, the 1936 amendments of the Indian Reorganization Act authorized the secretary of the interior to establish reservations, and Secretary Harold Ickes, a leading

New Dealer of President Roosevelt's administration, was favorably disposed
to wield this power on behalf of Alaska Natives. Second, as ANB leaders
were beginning to realize, reservations had been the only means by which
other Native Americans had retained ownership, however qualified, to significant sections of land. Furthermore, the Annette Island Reservation, a
Tsimshian enclave southwest of Ketchikan, served as a model that proved
the concept could be successfully applied to Alaska.

One problem with the reservation concept was that it offended Tlingit
and Haida aspirations to self-determination. For most ANB members, the
prospect of becoming "reservation Indians" meant subjugating themselves
to the authority of the Office of Indian Affairs. Southeast Alaska Natives
were intensely proud of their independence from government control and
preferred to think of themselves as "free Indians."[103]

The stubborn insistence on independence can be found in the sen-
timents recorded during the April 9, 1941, meeting in Wrangell of the
Tlingit-Haida Claims Committee. During the meeting, political oppo-
sites Roy Peratrovich and William Paul expressed their common views:
"I don't think that there is a man in this room that would stand for the
Office of Indian Affairs to dictate to us," Peratrovich said when addressing
the topic of how to organize the lawsuit allowed for by the Jurisdictional
Act of 1935. William Paul, taking up the discussion, admitted that
Peratrovich had "just about taken my speech away from me." Paul went on
to say: "Never by a single word shall I concede a single right that belongs
to me. . . . I will have nothing to do with this suit if the record shows that
there is some control over us by the Office of Indian Affairs."[104]

There was nothing surprising about Peratrovich and Paul's shared attitudes. The self-reliance of Southeast Alaska Natives had long been recognized, a characteristic that Sheldon Jackson and his fellow Presbyterians
promoted for purposes Professor Langdon believes were more calculat-
ing and political than benign. He suggests that the missionaries began
referring to the indigenous people of Southeast as "Alaska Natives" so
that their Native students and congregants would consciously separate
themselves from the "reservation Indians" of the Lower Forty-eight.
Nevertheless, the term *Alaska Native* is, in modern parlance, entirely
positive and remains a practical shorthand that encompasses all groups
indigenous to Alaska. Independence from government oversight remains
a point of pride.[105]

In 1930, Alaska's delegate to Congress, Dan Sutherland, was quoted as saying of Alaska Natives: "They are not wards of the government of the United States; they are absolutely a free people and have never yet been...under the supervision of the Bureau of Indian Affairs....The Native people of Alaska do not want to come under this bureau. They live in dread of it."[106]

Southeast Alaska Natives of this era equated reservations with imprisonment, wardship, and corruption. By the late 1930s, letters and testimony began to liken reservations to concentration camps, one of those allusions, like the much-later-coined "bridge to nowhere," that exerted an insurmountable negative connotation.[107]

During the 1941 Tlingit-Haida Claims Committee meeting, William Paul provided this succinct history of Indian reservations:

> [The] earliest reservations that were established were military reservations and concerned Indians who were placed on reservations in the condition of prisoners of war. Then the Indian problem passed through a phase where control was turned over to civilian agents. Contracts were let by companies in which the agents themselves had interests, or their relatives, and a great deal of corruption came in that manner.[108]

Reservations had one undeniable appeal to the ANB leadership: they had been the only means by which Native Americans succeeded in securing Indian title to land and waters that could then be exclusively used by Natives. All other alternatives involved recompense for lands that had been taken. Even more appealing to Southeast Alaska Natives, establishing reservations meant taking control of surrounding ocean waters and resources, as did the Tsimshians on the Annette Island Reservation who, to this day, exercise exclusive control to waters along a three-thousand-foot perimeter extending seaward from the shoreline around the island.

During the 1940s, the ANB leadership began to imagine a type of Native reserve that would retain the benefits of exclusive land rights and control of fisheries along the shoreline but preserve political autonomy free from federal bureaucratic control.

Joe Kahklen Sr. of Kake, a grade-school teacher and a Tlingit fluent in his native language (he served as translator for Walter Goldschmidt and Theodore Hass during field research for the 1946 land claims report "Possessory Rights of the Natives of Southeastern Alaska"), captured the essence of the idealized reserve in a letter to Bill Paul Jr. in 1946:

> If I have the information right, before our people [Indians] can claim legally any section of land collectively through aboriginal ownership, we must first file a petition requesting same and which must be approved by the Secretary of the Interior. Such land when set aside would be called a "reserve." This land to be used exclusively by our people to further their economic livelihood, etc. I also know that such a move or an act on our part would not change or endanger our present status of citizenship. It seems to me under such a plan, we have everything to gain and nothing to lose; but we must act collectively and immediately if our demands are to be met with favorable results....Like so many of our people I personally dislike the term "reservation" but look what it has done for Metlakatla....These people will continue for generations to come to draw on the natural resource of this land that has been set aside for them.[109]

Efforts to establish reservations in Alaska met with early success due to the support of top Interior Department officials in Washington, D.C., who clearly favored creating large reserves to protect Alaska Native lands and subsistence resources.[110]

In 1943, Secretary of the Interior Harold Ickes created by fiat huge reservations at Venetie, north of the Yukon River and near the border with Canada, and at Karluk on Kodiak Island, setting off widespread protests by politicians, industry representatives, and many federal officials of affected agencies in the territory of Alaska. Despite the protests, Ickes proposed, several months later, to create three additional reserves surrounding the Southeast villages of Kake, Klawock, and Hydaburg, primarily to protect fishing rights.

The specter of Natives reclaiming exclusive rights to land in Southeast mobilized the opposition of timber interests, which had just begun planning the development of a pulp industry in the region. But the most vehement opposition came from a fish processing industry that feared the potential loss of salmon resources in coastal waters.

W. C. Arnold, a lawyer for the salmon canning industry, attacked the reservation concept in the *Alaska Fishing News* in September 1944: "if the [Indians'] claims were recognized, it would result in the confiscation of a major portion of the salmon industry in Southeast Alaska."[111]

In the fall of 1944, Secretary Ickes appointed Justice Richard Hanna[112] to conduct hearings in Klawock and Seattle on the proposed Southeast Alaska reservations. Ickes directed Hanna to determine the "extent of Indian lands which should be protected by new legislation aimed at regulating Alaska fisheries."[113]

The transcripts of the hearings provide fascinating reading. Alaska Natives, many elderly, testified to their long and continued use and occupancy of land in Southeast, describing their semimigratory lifestyle to hunt, fish, and trap during the various seasons. Their testimony also described how the fishing industry's use of fish traps had circumscribed Alaska Natives' participation in commercial fishing.

The testimony of George Edward Haldane, a Haida, provides insight into the Alaska Native perception of negative intent of federally imposed fishing regulations. Haldane recounted how federal regulations had made it illegal to fish in streams, a traditional means by which Alaska Natives harvested salmon for subsistence purposes. He testified that Natives discovered new methods of "hooking off" (tying one end of a seine net to shore, an early commercial fishing technique), commenting that by doing so "we were getting along fine." Government regulations required commercial fishermen to report, upon delivery of their catch, where the fish had been caught. "After several years of this system of catching fish," Haldane said, "the [industrial] traps were erected just exactly where we reported that we catched the fish from."[114]

Those favorable to the cannery interests used the opportunity afforded by the Hanna hearings to mobilize opposition to the reserve concept. According to Stephen Haycox, certain business interests

> felt the reserves would retard if not make entirely impossible the progress of the fishing industry, and the development of Alaska at all. Alaska's Governor Gruening was among those opposed to reserves. Natives were in the way of progress, some witnesses implied, and reservations would lock them into place forever to stunt Alaska's

growth. Such views created an atmosphere oppressive to
many Natives.[115]

Meanwhile, William Paul Sr. sponsored a resolution at the 1944 Grand
Camp convention in Kake that praised Ickes for his help but disavowed
reservations as the solution to the Native land question. Paul instead favored legislation that would first transfer title to lands being directly used
by Natives at that time, primarily land within village boundaries, as well
as fish camps, smokehouse sites, and other areas; and second, provide
compensation for the lands in Southeast that had previously been taken
by government action. Although there is no direct link between this reso-

*By the 1930s when this photo was taken of fishermen working a seine boat, salmon cannery
interests had consolidated control of fisheries, forcing independent commercial fishermen out
of the most productive areas. During the Hanna hearings in 1944, a Native fisherman spoke
of canneries taking advantage of government reporting requirements to find the ideal locations for traps in salmon-rich coastal areas long used by Native fishermen. After a trap was
licensed and in place, seiners, trollers, and other commercial fishermen were then prohibited from fishing near the trap. The concentration of wealth and political power with cannery
owners, and the distant control of fisheries by federal bureaucrats, stoked broad resentment
among Alaskans. Abolishing fish traps became a primary goal of the Alaska statehood movement. Photo courtesy of the Andrew Hope III collection.*

lution and the Alaska Native Claims Settlement Act of 1971, it is interesting to note that the aspiration to receive private fee simple title to defined tracts of land, and compensation for land taken, would constitute the essence of the future settlement.

While the resolution passed by majority vote at the 1944 convention, it did not have the support of Frank G. Johnson, an important leader from Kake, who had previously opposed reservations and argued against the resolution. He voiced his concern that anti-Native forces would exploit the apparent disunity within the ANB on the question of reserves. Johnson, reflecting the shift of attitude that was taking place in the Native community toward "reserves" free of control by the Office of Indian Affairs, expressed his opinion that "it would be a tragic mistake to not ask for reservations" because reservations might be the only opportunity Alaska Natives would have to reclaim land.[116]

The subsequent Hanna Report, issued in the spring of 1945, recommended that only small tracts of land and limited waters be held in reserve. Judge Hanna's decision satisfied neither the supporters of reservations nor the opponents. In any event, his recommendations would be ignored by the new secretary of the interior, Julius "Cap" Krug (serving under President Harry S. Truman). Illustrating the stubborn independence of the people indigenous to Southeast Alaska, in December 1946, the village of Klukwan rejected the Department of the Interior's approval of a ninety-five-thousand acre reservation that the village itself had petitioned for in 1943. As Haycox notes, "They had thought in 1943 that the reservation would include full title to the land. When they learned that this was untrue, and that the reservation land would be held in trust for them by the Interior Department, they rejected the specter of Indian Office control."[117]

At the 1947 ANB Grand Camp convention at Hydaburg, the membership voted in favor of a 100,001-acre reservation encompassing the Haida community. Secretary of Interior Krug, on November 30, 1949, his last day in office, signed the paperwork that approved the Hydaburg Indian Reservation.[118]

The reservation issue did not appear to ignite passionate debate among the Alaska Native Brotherhood's general membership so much as spark disagreements over strategy among the organization's leadership, as former Central Council president Edward K. Thomas explains:

> They knew that the people they represented did not really want to live on a single reservation but they also knew that if they were ever going to get land back or get compensated for the loss of aboriginal land title or both they could not tolerate language in any legislation prohibiting Indian reservations. Unappealing as they were to Alaska Natives, reservations were the accepted methodology of dealing with aboriginal land issues by the government of the United States.[119]

In hearings held in Washington, D.C., during February 1950, Delegate Bartlett, consistently sympathetic to Alaska Native interests, stated his opposition to reservations in Southeast:

> Now it is said that these won't be typical or customary reservations, as we know them in the States; they will be a different kind entirely. But I submit that when [Alaska Natives] aren't given the land and when, in addition, they aren't even allowed to cut the timber without the permission of another agency of the Federal Government on the land ostensibly handed to them, they are going to find their lives in every particular pretty seriously circumscribed.[120]

Again, we note a conceptual framework consistent with the later settlement—ANCSA—conveying land to Alaska Natives free of the heavy hand of paternalistic government agencies.

Even though in retrospect it may seem difficult to square Bartlett's reputation as being empathetic to Alaska Natives with his steadfast opposition to reservations, he was adhering to his principles. Annette Island was but the exception to the rule: reservations in the Lower Forty-eight were sinks of poverty, ill health, unemployment, and want. Like many New Dealers, Bartlett, an unrepentant assimilationist, believed in the melting pot theory of social dynamics that had worked for the array of immigrants who had flooded through the gates of Ellis Island. An outspoken opponent of segregation, he believed the end result of reservations would be a division of the races in Alaska.[121]

A pocket park in Metlakatla within the Annette Island Reserve, 2004. During the ANB's consideration of reservations as a means to own land and resources, Metlakatla, well run and relatively prosperous, contradicted the common perception that reservations were the equivalent of Indian concentration camps. Photo by Peter Metcalfe.

"Now the very same people who tell us that reservations in the United States have failed dismally are trying to convince us that reservations are the only answer for Alaska," Bartlett said in a floor speech in Congress: "I grieve that these people, the most of whom are so well intentioned, have not gone to the trouble of learning the facts."[122]

The Alaska reservation movement fell victim to obstructionists within the Alaska Office of Indian Affairs; contrary judicial opinions; intense opposition by the salmon canning, mining, and logging interests of the day; and a lack of political support even from politicians friendly to Alaska Natives. But more than anything, the concept of reservations lacked the support of the ANB rank and file, in part because of their fear that residency in reservations could mean losing their hard-won rights of citizenship.

Elizabeth Peratrovich and Frank G. Johnson, two leaders in the ANB's campaign to end discrimination, enjoy a dance at an ANB/ANS function, circa 1946. In the early 1930s, Johnson had led a successful effort to desegregate Juneau movie theaters, and Elizabeth and her husband, Roy, were at the forefront of the effort that led to the signing of the Anti-Discrimination Act in 1945. During the second half of the 1940s, the ANB/ANS began to seriously consider reservations as a means of reclaiming title to land and ownership of fish and game. Working against this concept was the widespread feeling among Alaska Natives that reservations seemed a step back to a segregated society, especially just after the civil rights victory. Photo courtesy of Sealaska Heritage Institute, William Paul Jr. collection.

The denouement of the Alaska reservation movement came in 1952, when George W. Folta, federal district judge for Alaska, invalidated the establishment of the Hydaburg Indian Reservation, ruling in favor of a salmon canning company. As Robert Price notes, "After sixteen years of contention, the one reservation established in Southeast Alaska under the Indian Reorganization Act was ordered out of existence."[123]

The election of Dwight Eisenhower later that year ushered in a conservative Republican administration. While the secretary of the interior retained the right to establish new reservations in Alaska, the authority would not be exercised for the duration of the Eisenhower administration, nor ever again. As a final note on the reservation question, Price observes that in 1976 "an obscure provision of the Federal Land Policy Management Act repealed the authority of the Secretary [of Interior] to establish Indian reservations under the Indian Reorganization Act."[124]

Although the postwar efforts to establish reservations in Alaska failed, there were consequences: the people most deeply involved in the Alaska statehood movement came to realize that aboriginal rights actually existed and that Native claims remained unsettled. Over the next couple of years, attempts would be made to settle these claims once and for all.

Members of the last territorial legislature who had also been elected to the first Alaska State Legislature assembled for their portrait in 1959. Then, as now, the legislature included twenty senators and forty representatives. Four Alaska Native members were elected to serve in the first state legislature, including Frank Peratrovich and Andrew Hope, standing second and third from the left, and Eben Hopson, kneeling third from right. Aside from those in this photo, the only other Alaska Native in the first Alaska State Legislature, John Nusunginya of Point Barrow, had just been elected to his first term. Photo courtesy of the Alaska State Historical Library.

5

A Bad Time for Indians

In the immediate aftermath of World War II, statehood for Alaska rose to the surface along with many other long-deferred national issues. The territory's leading politicians, Gov. Ernest Gruening and Alaska's nonvoting delegate to Congress, E. L. "Bob" Bartlett, made statehood their top priority. Although there had been earlier attempts to bring the territory of Alaska into the Union, it was the postwar effort that gained momentum, finally succeeding when President Eisenhower signed the Alaska Statehood Bill in 1958.

In 1950, Alaska's population of 128,643 had nearly doubled from the previous census, but the population of Alaska Natives had increased only slightly (less than 5 percent since 1940) and, in that year, represented about a quarter of the territory's population. By the time Alaska achieved statehood, the total population had again almost doubled, yet again the Native population increased only modestly, then representing about one-fifth of the total population, a ratio that decreased slightly in the decades that followed.[125]

Although Natives represented a quarter of the population in the immediate postwar era, they constituted less than 10 percent of the territorial legislature during the time of the statehood movement. Of the fifty-five delegates to the Alaska Constitutional Convention in Fairbanks (held in the winter of 1955–1956), only one, Frank Peratrovich, was an Alaska Native.

Through the 1950s and the first decade of statehood, very few Alaska Natives were to be found in executive positions anywhere outside of federal employment. Almost as rare were Alaska Natives working in midlevel white-collar and clerical positions. Racial prejudice remained a fact of life for Alaska Natives. Nonetheless, Alaska Natives were not ignored. Delegate Bartlett, who held the only territory-wide elected position, remained loyal to his Alaska Native constituents, from whom he could count on strong electoral support.[126]

Describing Bartlett's first election in 1944 as Alaska's delegate, Don Mitchell writes: "Bartlett's early views on the settlement of Alaska Native land claims reflected an empathy that transcended the prejudice of the society of which he now was a leader."[127]

In the years 1945 to 1958, Alaska Native leaders observed the statehood movement with mixed feelings, acutely aware that the transfer of Alaska from federal to local control would bring about major changes.

Up to that time, Alaska Natives had had an unhappy relationship with the federal government, which had assumed a trust relationship similar to that for Native Americans in the Lower 48.[128] All too often, Native Americans who found themselves dependent in any way on government services were subjected to rude and condescending supervision. Worse yet, especially for Alaska Natives who had no alternatives, the services provided fell far below the standards of similar services available to the non-Native population, and nowhere was this discrimination more obvious than in the provision of health care. In the early 1950s, the exposure of the federal government's failure to address the tuberculosis epidemic in Alaska Native villages became a national scandal.[129]

On the other hand, the federal government was the devil they knew. Would Alaska Natives be better off with the government of a new state in the control of their non-Native neighbors?

It bears remembering that, for Alaska Natives, Alaska during the statehood movement was very different from Alaska of today, when even the most racially insensitive feel compelled to preface their transparently racist remarks with "I am not a racist, but..." In the immediate postwar era, outspoken and unqualified contempt for Natives was commonplace.

Although the basic tenets of citizenship had been acquired in the 1920s, racial discrimination remained legal until 1945 when the Anti-Discrimination Act became law—the culmination of a long and vigorous lobbying effort by members of the Alaska Native Brotherhood and Sisterhood. No legislation could overcome ingrained racism, a word by then in common use, but the new law did begin the process of ending the worst aspects of racial discrimination. An Alaska legislator when the proposed law was debated in the Alaska territorial legislature noted that larceny, rape, and murder were illegal, but that did not stop those crimes. Elizabeth Peratrovich replied, "No law will eliminate crimes, but at least you, as legislators, can assert to the world that you recognize the evil of the present situation and speak your intent to help us overcome discrimination."[130]

If there was a single issue that all Alaskans, most enthusiastically Natives of Southeast Alaska, could rally around, it was fish traps—not the

In this now-iconic photograph, Elizabeth Peratrovich and her husband, Roy (far right), observe Governor Ernest Gruening signing the Anti-Discrimination Act on February 16, 1945, along with Sen. O. D. Cochran (far left) and Rep. Edward Anderson (center), both of Nome, and Sen. Norman "Doc" Walker (second from right) of Ketchikan. The Peratroviches, who dedicated their lives to winning equality for Alaska Natives, rightly deserve their place of prominence among the many Alaskans who worked to achieve equal rights, liberty, and justice for all. Photo courtesy of the Alaska Historical Library.

river traps on which Alaskans who lived along the interior river systems depended but the large, industrial traps, hundreds of which lined Alaska's coasts, trapping migratory salmon by the tens of millions. A majority of Alaskans perceived a strong link between statehood and the abolition of fish traps.

The Native people of Southeast—Tlingit, Haida, and Tsimshian—largely depended on the fisheries for their livelihoods. The widespread perception was that fish traps, most of which were owned and controlled by corporations based outside of Alaska, were preventing Alaska Natives from making a reasonable living in fisheries.

In 1953, at the age of twelve, Edward K. Thomas began working on a seine boat out of Craig during the summers. "Not only were the fish traps consuming a lot of fish, but they were [causing] an all around price reduction for troll-caught and seine-caught fish," he explains.[131]

Throughout its history, the Alaska Native Brotherhood repeatedly passed resolutions requesting the abolition of fish traps. Many, perhaps most, Alaska Natives in Southeast considered the promised abolition of fish traps to be a good enough reason to support statehood.

But for the statehood movement to gain traction, the first barrier to be surmounted was the Republican-controlled Eighty-third Congress (1953–1954). In those years, Alaska was firmly in the Democratic camp and would surely elect Democrats to Congress. Added to that, Dwight David Eisenhower, supreme Allied commander in Europe during the final eighteen months of World War II, had won the presidency in November 1952. The military, and apparently Eisenhower himself, favored keeping the strategically important Alaska a federal fiefdom.[132]

Complicating matters for the Alaska Native Brotherhood, conservative interests (including southern Democrats) that might otherwise be persuaded to support adding Alaska to the Union were generally opposed to aboriginal rights. The hammer close at hand to deal with such claims was "termination," the movement to eliminate the special relationship between the federal government and Native Americans.

The first years of the Eisenhower administration would mark the high-water line of the termination movement, a period during which attempts, some successful, were made in Congress to unwind the nearly cen-

The political consequences of the Cold War worked against Alaska Native claims, which many national policy makers considered detrimental to national security. Photo courtesy of the Alaska Historical Library.

tury and a half of constitutional law and federal regulations concerning Native Americans.

Termination is now largely recalled in the context of the disbanding of many tribes, but the larger objective of ending the government-to-government relationship with tribes extended to postwar Alaska in the form of efforts to abolish aboriginal claims.

In the years between the two world wars, Alaska moved into the center of the national consciousness as military leaders came to realize its strategic importance. By the time the statehood movement had truly begun, in 1946, the Iron Curtain had descended across Europe and the threat of Communism promised to become the overwhelming geopolitical issue facing the United States. This was at the dawn of the nuclear era, by which time Alaska's geostrategic significance was fully appreciated.[133]

The termination movement, influenced by the strong sense of American exceptionalism that pervaded the country following World

War II, was founded on the belief that all Native Americans would do best by assimilating—a belief that in its most benign form recognized Native Americans as individuals with full rights of citizenship who would be far better off freed from the paternalistic grasp of often incompetent and sometimes corrupt federal bureaucrats. If Indians and Alaska Natives were fully assimilated, there would be no need for tribes.

At the far right of America's political spectrum, termination was favored because, among other things, the very concept of tribalism seemed quasi-communistic and contrary to a financial system rooted in a capitalist freemarket economy.

To those who, for whatever reason, favored the termination of the federal relationship with tribes, recognition of Alaska Natives' aboriginal claims seemed a step backward and, considering Alaska's geostrategic significance, potentially detrimental to the military security of the United States.

It was within this context that legislation to define and resolve aboriginal claims in Alaska began to receive serious attention.

The termination movement, never entirely absent from the inner sanctums of the federal government, crested in 1953 with the introduction of House Concurrent Resolution 108, which officially established tribal termination as the country's Indian policy:

> [I]t is the policy of Congress . . . to make the Indians within the territorial limits of the United States subject to the same laws and entitled to the same privileges and responsibilities as are applicable to other citizens of the United States, to end their status as wards of the United States, and to grant them all the rights and prerogatives pertaining to American citizenship.[134]

The legislation, which Congress passed on August 1, 1953, terminated the federal government's special relationship with all tribes in California, Florida, New York, and Texas, and specific tribes in Montana, Oregon, Wisconsin, Kansas, and Nebraska—more than one hundred tribes in all, or about 3 percent of all Native Americans.[135] The terminated tribes lost their legal status and some ceased to exist.

The momentum of the termination movement slowed when Democrats reclaimed control of Congress in January 1955. Eventually termination fell out of favor, but not before emptying many reservations and scattering thousands of Native Americans into the lonely poverty of urban slums without the comfort of their extended families or any meaningful connection with their heritage.[136]

The momentum to put an end to the aboriginal claims of Alaska Natives also slowed, but only after the ANB and its allies faced down and stopped the several serious attempts, beginning as early as 1947, to find a quick or cheap resolution to extinguish or abolish those claims.

Choke setters working a clearcut in Rowan Bay on Kuiu Island, part of the fifty-year sale that sustained the Sitka pulp mill. The Tongass Timber Act of 1947 got the ball rolling for the postwar timber industry in Southeast Alaska. While the bill resolved nothing for the Native people of the region, it did provide for an escrow account that would hold all timber proceeds received by the government until such time as Native rights to the land and timber were resolved. However indirectly, the provision admitted there were issues to settle regarding "Indian title" in Alaska. Photo by Peter Metcalfe.

6

The Extinguishment Legislation

The ANB's success in convincing Congress to grant the Tlingit and Haida people jurisdiction to pursue their claims in 1935—and then, a year later, to extend the Indian Reorganization Act to Alaska—had consequences that were to play out during the first phase of the statehood movement.

Section 2 of the 1936 Indian Reorganization Act gave Interior Secretary Ickes the power to create reservations in Alaska. When he exercised that power, his actions provoked widespread protests, prompting the 1944 Hanna hearings on the possessory claims of Alaska Natives.

In 1946, the Tlingit-Haida Central Council, accepting a compromise brokered by Felix Cohen, contracted with James Curry, an attorney then working for the National Congress of American Indians (NCAI, established in 1944), to pursue the Tlingit and Haida lawsuit. A year later, Curry filed *Tlingit and Haida Indians v. United States* in the U.S. Court of Claims.

All of this raised the awareness of political and business leaders of all persuasions that Alaska aboriginal title was an issue yet to be settled. Until these claims were resolved, uncertainties surrounding land ownership would cast a shadow over the nascent Southeast Alaska pulpwood industry, threaten the salmon canning industry's dominance of commercial fisheries in Alaska, and present a barrier to statehood.

The solution favored by pro-timber interests was to have Congress pass legislation that would allow the Forest Service to sell timber "regardless of whether the land on which the trees were located was subject to aboriginal title."[137] As Stephen Haycox explains:

After World War II the Alaska regional forest director pursued aggressively a plan to develop as many as five major pulp mills in the Tongass Forest. Forest Service bureaucrats discounted the notion of aboriginal title, arguing that the most land in the archipelago Indians might be entitled to was that which their dwellings occupied.[138]

The Tongass Timber Act was drafted to allow timber contracts to proceed. The Alaska Native Brotherhood, fearful that this legislation would compromise its claims, sent Frank Johnson, Andrew Hope, Fred Grant (a Haida leader), and Frank Peratrovich to Washington, D.C., to testify against the bill in 1947.[139]

The opposition by these Alaska Natives to the legislation did not stop its enactment just before Congress went into summer recess in late July of 1947. But the presence in Washington of articulate Alaska Native advocates lobbying for aboriginal title helped move the issue onto the national stage. Under the authority of the new legislation, the U.S. Forest Service signed a fifty-year contract with the Ketchikan Pulp and Paper Company for 8.25 billion board feet of timber. The bill required, however, that the proceeds from timber sales be deposited in a special account "until the [Natives'] rights to the land and timber are finally determined."[140]

Earlier in the same year that the Tongass Timber Act became law, Bob Bartlett introduced the first Alaska statehood bill to be taken seriously, H.R. 206. It failed to mention Alaska Native claims.

James Curry, testifying before Congress on behalf of the Tlingit-Haida Central Council, spoke to the absence of any treatment of aboriginal title in Bartlett's statehood bill. He noted that statehood bills for other western states included a standard disclaimer clause by which the citizens of the new state would disavow all rights to lands acquired by the U.S. government that may have been held by Native Americans. These provisions, he said, "are universal in the western statehood bills providing for the protection of Indian property rights." Curry warned that without the provision, the Alaska Native Brotherhood, the National Congress of American Indians, and their allies would oppose the bill.[141]

This led to a series of extinguishment bills that attempted to clear title to the lands of Alaska in order to answer the concerns of industry and open the way for statehood: H.R. 7002 (introduced in June 1948), H.R. 4388 (June 1951), and H.R. 1921 (January 1953).

For Alaska Natives of that period, extinguishment legislation—settlement of Alaska Native claims by another name—was a means of receiving compensation for what they had already lost and title to land they used and occupied. Most politicians engaged in the debate over the extinguishment bills agreed that Alaska Natives should be granted legal title to some land, as well as some compensation, but how many acres of land, under what conditions, and how much money were points of disagreement.

A key provision of H.R. 7002 (introduced in 1948) authorized the secretary of the interior to convey legal title to Alaska Natives for limited amounts of land used and occupied "for towns, villages, buildings, smoke houses, cultivated fields or gardens, hunting or fishing camps, burial grounds, missionary stations, meeting places, or other improvements."[142] While few contested that Alaska Natives deserved title to such lands, a major sticking point that persisted throughout the consideration of each extinguishment bill was what to do about land that, depending on one's perspective, had either been "seized" by the government or "abandoned" by the Natives. Were Alaska Natives due compensation for or title to land they no longer used or occupied—even if they had been forced or ordered off the land?

Alaska Natives and their allies looked upon "abandonment" as a transparent excuse to legalize the seizure of Native property. Federal agencies had long ignored "use and occupancy" by Alaska Natives on widely dispersed lands where they tended gardens, harvested berries and greens, established seasonal fish camps, and hunted and trapped.

In few areas was the uncompensated taking of property rights more obvious than in Southeast Alaska, where the U.S. Forest Service ignored use by Natives of land on islands to which the agency granted exclusive-use permits to non-Native fox farmers. The ANB leadership and their attorneys and advisors held to the belief that absent a treaty or congressional action the taking of land by the government had "extinguished" aboriginal title, and for this reason Alaska Natives deserved to be compensated.

Since the extinguishment legislation would recognize that by conveying title or use rights to others the federal government had extinguished aboriginal title, ANB leaders focused their attention on how or if the government intended to provide compensation. By July 1947, the Tongass Timber Act had become law, and few Alaska Natives, certainly none of the leaders, harbored hopes of reclaiming most of the land of Southeast Alaska. But there existed the options of establishing reservations and attaining title to lands long used for subsistence purposes—at least those lands not subject to timber sales, mining claims, or the existing title of private interests and municipalities. How the extinguishment legislation would affect reservations and land used and occupied by Alaska Natives focused the attention of ANB leaders.

According to Delegate Bob Bartlett, the authors of the first extinguishment bill, H.R. 7002, did not believe aboriginal possessory rights existed in areas other than land then used and occupied. The drafters of the legislation focused on lands surrounding villages, while Bartlett clearly felt aboriginal claims deserved to be more expansive. H.R. 7002 did allow Alaska Natives to claim lands village residents would need to "maintain an adequate standard of living"; yet this seemingly realistic and forward-thinking provision was rendered distasteful to Alaska Natives because any such additional land would be held in trust by the Forest Service and was considered less than generous since the U.S. would retain the subsurface estate.[143]

Under the terms of H.R. 7002 (as initially drafted), each community of Natives, as well as individual Natives, would have to file suit in U.S. District Court to obtain compensation for lands.[144] This provision added another complication: how would the attorneys needed to fight these legal battles be compensated?

James Curry and his NCAI allies, joined by several "friends of Indians" organizations, aggressively opposed H.R. 7002 on the grounds that its principal aim, the extinguishment of aboriginal title, would be accomplished on unfair terms. Joining in opposition was the National Advisory Committee on Indian Affairs, an eleven-member group appointed by the secretary of the interior.

When the issue reached President Truman's office, the opposition that Curry and his allies had stirred up convinced Truman, who considered himself a friend to Native Americans, to speak against the extinguishment legislation. "I have been informed," Truman wrote to his secretary of the interior, Julius Krug, "that one of the problems holding back the development of Alaska has been the matter of unresolved Native claims. Legislation has been proposed which is not satisfactory and which should not be passed."[145]

In response to Truman's objections, H.R. 7002 was revised, but Congress did not concur and the legislation was dropped early in 1950.

Up until 1950, all of Bob Bartlett's efforts to procure serious consideration for a statehood bill had been stymied by Republicans, who were certain that Alaskans would elect Democrats to the U.S. Senate. At the beginning of the year, however, Speaker of the House Sam Rayburn (D-TX), circumvented the rules that had conspired to mothball Alaska statehood bills. In March 1950, the Alaska statehood bill (H.R. 331) passed the House. But again, as with the 1947 bill, a disclaimer clause maintaining

A waterfront view of Hoonah in the early 1960s. While most Southeast Alaska Native villages had modernized in the postwar era, they still clustered at the edge of the sea and the people remained largely dependent on natural resources for their livelihoods and subsistence. Legislation that offered title to villages did not address the larger issue: the surrounding land and resources Natives used for subsistence purposes. Hoonah serves as a classic example of the Catch-22 in the debate over "occupancy." The people of Hoonah were excluded by agency (National Park Service) regulations from their subsistence grounds (Glacier Bay National Park); however, their subsequent absence was taken as evidence that they had abandoned the area. Photo courtesy of Sealaska Heritage Institute, William Paul Jr. collection.

Alaska Natives' land rights was omitted, sparking James Curry to rally opposition once again. Don Mitchell describes what happened next: "In June the stink Curry generated accomplished its objective when the Committee on Interior and Insular Affairs released a second draft of its statehood bill into which the Native land rights disclaimer section had been reinserted."[146]

Senator Hugh Butler (R-MT) tossed a poison pill into the mix when he amended the statehood bill to revoke existing reservations in Alaska and repeal the interior secretary's authority to create new ones. Butler was as much an opponent of statehood for Alaska (he believed Alaska would not have sufficient revenues to support a state government) as he was of aboriginal rights.

Native American rights supporters again rallied to the cause. Former Interior Secretary (1933–1946) Harold Ickes wrote to Secretary of the Interior (1950–1953) Oscar Chapman that it was "a particular shock to me that this further effort is being made to deprive the Indians of Alaska who are entitled [to] their immemorial property rights." He described the amendment as a "raid on the property" of Alaska Natives. On the same day, Ickes wrote a letter to Senator Joe Mahoney (D-WY) in which he explained why he felt it important to retain the option of establishing reservations in Alaska:

> The theory of permitting the Indians of Alaska...with their consent...to set up reservations was evolved by the Bureau of Indian Affairs when I was Secretary of the Interior....We could think of no other way in which to stop whittling away, not only the Indians' property, but their fishing and other rights....But what really shook me is your statement, "Alaska natives are citizens of the U.S. and ought to be treated as such." They have never been regarded, except in individual instances, as better than second or third-class citizens. Prior to the Roosevelt administration, Indians were being given individual property rights [a reference to the Dawes Act of 1887], under the pretense of putting them on a footing with white citizens and making them equal and independent. This was just a subterfuge for robbing the Indians blind.[147]

When the next ANB/ANS Grand Camp convention convened in Craig in November 1950, the antireservation provision remained a hot topic. James Curry and Governor Gruening, addressing the convention delegates on separate days, presented opposing views on reservations and aboriginal claims.[148]

Curry began his remarks by recognizing his co-counsels, Bill Paul Jr. and Clarence Lindquist, and describing their assignment by the Tlingit-Haida Central Council (in practice, the ANB Grand Camp executive committee), which was to obtain title through "reservation orders" to "certain land and waters [Southeast Natives] still own" and to obtain "payment through the Court of Claims for lands and waters that have been taken from the Indians in the past." By "owned," Curry was referring to land set aside for reservations.

It was Curry's opinion that the fight over the reservation question was entering its final phase. He warned his audience to reject Delegate Bartlett and Gov. Gruening's views on reservations.

On the topic of statehood, Curry strongly advised the ANB delegates to oppose "the present version of the Statehood Bill" (H.R. 331).

In his address two days later, Governor Gruening failed to get an accurate read on his audience. The governor's role in winning civil rights for Alaska Natives would command their respect throughout his political career, but in this speech, he demonstrated insensitivity to Native aspirations. He disparaged reservations "as a step backward" that would create a class system and dismissed Native efforts to reclaim land by implying that within a reservation their freedoms would be circumscribed; even though they might not own any land without reservations, they would be "completely free." Gruening advised his audience to "stop pursuing the reservation title myth and go after [compensation for] aboriginal claims to lands the title of which has already been lost." When asked pointed questions from the audience, Gruening was unprepared. In an attempt to play on Native fears of becoming wards of the government, he used the Annette Island Reserve as an example. A member of the audience corrected him by explaining that the Tsimshians of Metlakatla had adopted a quasi-independent form of tribal government under the terms of the Indian Reorganization Act.

Gruening simply did not believe Alaska Natives had special rights, aboriginal or otherwise; he believed they were citizens who enjoyed the same rights and privileges he himself enjoyed. It was this belief that had motivated Gruening's strong support for the Anti-Discrimination Act that he signed in 1945. While Gruening supported compensation for lost lands, he never supported efforts of Alaska Natives to reclaim title to any lands other than those that they actually occupied. Blinded perhaps by Curry's passionate embrace of reservations as the only practical means by which Natives could reclaim lands and rights, Gruening failed to appreciate that for most ANB leaders, the reservation option was a chit to be played, not an end unto itself.

The 1950 Grand Camp passed a resolution, introduced by Frank G. Johnson of Kake, by which the ANB resolved to "make every effort to get [the statehood] bill amended to conform with other recent Statehood Enabling Acts [by including a disclaimer clause,] and to eliminate the clause forbidding confirmation of Native land and water rights [i.e., blocking the authority to create reservations]." If they could not get a neutral

This Juneau dance group, formed in 1950, helped raise funds for a new local library. Most of the people pictured are identified on page 88 of the book In Sisterhood, *edited and produced by Kim Metcalfe. Photo courtesy of Kim Metcalfe.*

disclaimer clause in the statehood bill, Johnson recommended working to defeat the passage of that bill.[149]

A "Dear Senator" circular, written by James Curry on November 27, 1950, characterized the ANB's resolution as "anti-statehood" and stated that the resolution had passed the Grand Camp unanimously. In his letter, Curry explained that most Alaska Natives favored the statehood bill until the "joker" was inserted, "cheating them of their right to reserve for their own use any part of the lands that they inherited from their aboriginal ancestors." He went on to write:

> Gruening…spoke for hours, urging the Indians to forget about keeping land for themselves, as authorized by law, and to back the Statehood Bill. But the Indians adopted a resolution insisting on their rights and opposing any bill like the one now before the Senate, which limits or revokes the power to create such land reservations. In spite of Gruening's pleas, the vote on this resolution was unanimous.[150]

The following year, Governor Gruening's antireservation stance received another strong rebuke from the ANB, which, by unanimous resolution, opposed "any legislation which contains provisions limiting or abolishing the authority of federal officials to confirm Native land title as said Natives desire and are legally and equitably entitled to, whether by designation of reservations *or in any other manner*" (emphasis added).[151]

Neither Gruening nor Bartlett missed the point: they would lose the support of the ANB for any Alaska statehood bill that would appear to compromise Alaska Native rights.

*James Curry (left) and Al Willard at the 1950 ANB convention. In Fred Paul's estima
tion, Curry was "another unsung hero in the long history of our struggle." Photo courtesy of
Sealaska Heritage Institute, William Paul Jr. collection.*

7

Statehood or Native Claims

It would have been politically awkward for Bartlett to leave the issue of aboriginal title unresolved. By the 1950s, Native claims had come to be seen as an obstacle to industrial and economic development in Alaska and clearly stood as a barricade across the road to statehood. Yet Bartlett could not in good conscience abandon his loyal Alaska Native constituents. In June 1951, responding to a request by the Alaska territorial legislature, Bartlett introduced H.R. 4388, an extinguishment bill similar to H.R. 7002 except that it required Natives to assert legal title to land within two years of the projected effective date of the act. Although the bill allowed for future compensation, the abbreviated time line for claiming title alarmed Native leaders.

Those who supported Alaska Native claims were predisposed to oppose this legislation, which became known variously as the Possessory Claims Bill, the Bartlett Land Bill, and the Alaska Native Claims Bill. They may have taken some comfort, however, in the opposition to it by advocates of the brand-new Southeast Alaska timber industry. The assistant chief of the U.S. Forest Service "complained that the bill recognized a 'roving type' of Native use and occupancy that might be asserted 'to virtually' all the national forest land in southeastern Alaska."[152]

Depending on the amendments offered, this extinguishment legislation would gain and lose Native support over the next few years. William Paul and his "clique" (as his opponents characterized the Paul faction) appeared to support H.R. 4388, while James Curry and the Peratrovich contingent in the ANB opposed it. Reading the intensely combative letters between both sides during this period, it seems as if they were at loggerheads on the issue, when in fact one side would reluctantly support the bill with amendments, while the other side would remain implacable in its opposition unless the legislation were amended.[153]

At the November 1951 annual convention of the Alaska Native Brotherhood in Ketchikan, William Paul Sr. introduced a resolution demanding that H.R. 4388 be amended, arguing that "a failure on the part of Congress to adopt [the amendments] should entail the most vigorous opposition of this body and its friends."[154]

James Curry brought some clarity to the topic in testimony before the U.S. Senate on February 11, 1952. Describing the nature of his work as an attorney for the Tlingit and Haida people, he said, "We are not only trying to [get compensation] for them for the land taken, but also to defend the present right to the possession of that land that has not been taken."[155]

As Curry went on to explain, he meant compensation for Tongass National Forest lands that had been dedicated to other uses like logging or where private title had been conveyed; the "land that has not been taken" referred to all other Tongass lands, including that set aside by the secretary of the interior as reservations for Alaska Natives. Explaining the circumstances his clients found themselves in, Curry said:

> There isn't any provision of the law to file suit to get possession of land, [but] the Wheeler-Howard Act [a.k.a. the Indian Reorganization Act] provides the remedy under which the Secretary of the Interior may set aside land for these Indians. It is the same procedure…that was always used throughout the country from the very beginning. The only Indians that have ever gotten any land, if any of their land was left, were Indians who got reservations.…That is the way it has always been done.…That is the only way of doing it.[156]

By late 1952, Curry was dead set against any extinguishment legislation. In a hyperbolic circular to the ANB in October, he provided his clients a worst-case (and entirely unlikely) scenario: "[The] Bartlett Bill, which would have confiscated all your property, even including your houses…has been blocked [through] my efforts, coupled with those of the National Congress of American Indians, and in spite of the contrary efforts of William Paul Sr."[157]

William Paul Sr. responded to this circular by writing that the ANB executive committee "did not try to get this bill passed," and explained that in his testimony to the House committee he had said the ANB would support the bill only if it were amended.[158]

By this time, Curry was at the end of his rope, personally and professionally. In his book, *Then Fight for It*, Fred Paul recalls sharing dinner in Seattle with Curry, who was on his way to Alaska. Curry was so exhausted he fell asleep at the table.[159]

Despite the enmity between Curry and their father, Fred and Bill Paul appeared to have enjoyed a collegial working relationship with Curry. Fred Paul credits Curry for "heroic efforts on behalf of his clients," during which "he sustained many personal attacks.... Curry is another unsung hero in the long history of our struggle."[160]

By the close of 1952, Curry was no longer practicing Indian law. He blamed the Department of the Interior for undermining his law practice. Although there was more to the loss of his practice than Curry admitted, his assertion that federal bureaucrats conspired to deny Alaska Natives the right to representation by any lawyer other than those willing to be controlled by the Department of the Interior no doubt found a sympathetic ear with William Paul.[161]

To Curry belongs the lion's share of credit for mobilizing national opposition to congressional efforts adverse to Alaska Native interests. The National Congress of American Indians continued to support the Central Council, although without Curry as the organization's attorney and Alaska liaison. The Tlingit and Haida lawsuit that had brought Curry into the ANB's orbit had since been passed on to attorneys I. S. Weisbrodt and David Cobb, who litigated the case to conclusion.[162]

The fight to add amendments to extinguishment legislation continued, with the objectives of protecting Alaska Natives' right to fair compensation, gaining title to land "used and occupied," and retaining the reservation option. In a letter dated February 24, 1953, Bill Paul Jr. informed Grand Camp President Joe Williams that a new version of H.R. 4388 had been introduced as H.R. 1921 and that he generally supported it (so long as it was amended). Illustrating the ANB's internecine battles of the time, Peter C. Nielson, grand secretary, responded to the letter with a blistering attack on the Pauls, father and son, charging them with "apparent indifference to protect the fast diminishing rights of Alaska Indians."[163]

A resolution passed by the NCAI convention in 1953 requested that Congress hold more hearings on the legislation, noting that Alaska Natives had previously testified but that the bill had been significantly changed since then. "[Alaska] Natives have had no opportunity to express their views with respect to these additions, amendments, and the report of the Department of the Interior."[164]

During this period, Elizabeth Peratrovich[165] was serving as the ANB's liaison to the National Congress of American Indians while John Hope, Andrew's son, was serving as Grand Camp secretary. It appears the Hopes maintained a relatively neutral position in the Paul-Peratrovich feud in spite of William Paul's withering criticism of both Hopes, especially John Hope, to whom he addressed a stream of hectoring and condescending correspondence.[166]

The poisonous nature of the Paul-Peratrovich feud is illustrated by William Paul's description of an encounter at a Grand Camp convention:

> Frank Peratrovich nodded to me and I thought he smiled. I guess I was mistaken because at recess I went over to him and offered to shake hands with him as I have always done before and he said (as he sat) "No, I don't think I care to shake hands with you. You went just a little too far in this campaign, and so I think we might just as well be enemies." To this I replied, "Have we ever been friends?" and he answered, "I thought so." I then said, "You are a damn liar. You have never been a friend to me." He rose to his feet and said, "Don't you call me a liar or I'll slap your face and the other side too." I replied, "I have said it now, go ahead and slap. Go ahead. Slap both sides." And I stuck my chin out. He then said, "You are too old," and I countered, "I can take it." The scene ended there.[167]

Both sides of the ANB—the Peratroviches and the Pauls—agreed that the two-year time limit for asserting claims, first included in H.R. 4388, was entirely impractical. In spite of all the acrimony that filled their interactions and back-and-forth correspondence, there seemed to be general agreement that the latest iteration of the extinguishment legislation, H.R. 1921, with amendment, could be made to work for the benefit of Alaska Natives.

After his disbarment, William Paul Sr. relied on his sons, William ("Bill") Jr. (left), and Frederick, both of whom had received their law degrees in 1939, to continue his work on the Tlingit-Haida lawsuit. William later disassociated himself, taking another path by having Tee-Hit-Ton filed on behalf of his clan. Bill Paul, elected grand secretary of the ANB in 1939, went on to serve as an adjunct lawyer in the Tlingit and Haida lawsuit, which was filed in 1947. Photo, circa 1960s, courtesy of Ben Paul.

On November 30, 1953, Elizabeth Peratrovich wrote a letter to Helen Peterson, the NCAI executive director, requesting the organization's help. Demonstrating that the dispute between the Pauls and the Peratroviches reached beyond the family patriarchs, Elizabeth took a gratuitous swipe at Bill Paul Jr. as she asked a favor of Peterson: "Some of the members [of the ANB] do not have complete faith in the A.N.B. attorney, Wm. Paul Jr., and whatever you people can suggest on [H.R.] 1921 will be greatly appreciated. There is of course the possibility that the Interior Department may make further recommendations as to amendments to H.R. 1921."[168] Little did she know that the machinations of Washington bureaucrats were about to turn the extinguishment bill into Native claims elimination legislation.

In a circular to the Grand Camp executive committee dated January 5, 1954, William Paul's son Bill, the ANB's attorney, responded to the motion passed by the 1953 Grand Camp convention opposing H.R. 1921 "unless six points are adopted." The motion included a request that he make comments and suggestions regarding the requested amendments. The gist of his commentary was that most of the ANB's requested changes to H.R. 1921 would be received favorably, with the exception of one that insisted the authority of the secretary of the interior to create reservations be retained.[169] But the ANB's attempts to fit a square peg into a round hole had misled them into thinking H.R. 1921 could be refined to their advantage.

Judging from the correspondence regarding the bill, ANB leaders may have had some inkling that the Department of the Interior was working with the Department of Justice behind closed doors on amendments to H.R. 1921, although it is clear they were not aware that such changes would, as Mitchell writes, "preclude the United States from being required to compensate Alaska Natives for the extinguishment of their aboriginal title."[170] The revisions were so injurious that, had they been so informed, even William Paul Sr. and Frank Peratrovich would have found common cause in opposing the changes to what proved to be the last in the series of extinguishment legislation until the Alaska Native Claims Settlement Act of 1971.

In the first week of January 1954, Paul Sr. wrote to J. C. Peacock, the Washington, D.C., attorney who had filed the lawsuit on behalf of the Tee-Hit-Ton clan, informing him that he and Andrew Hope would be in the capital "for an indefinite stay to see if we cannot save [H.R. 1921]." In the letter, Paul expressed his ambivalence about the legislation: "We consider it wicked and unconscionable for a great and big government like ours to legislate a matter that should not be done except by a court." He then gets to the point, addressing the abandonment issue head on: "Our Indians were praised because they were 'peaceful' but now the very absence of bloodshed is used as proof that we (our ancestors) either didn't claim the land or else abandoned it to the johnny-come-latelys."[171]

After receiving a copy of Paul's letter to Peacock, Helen Peterson[172] of the NCAI wrote to Elizabeth Peratrovich and ANB Grand Secretary John Hope on January 22, 1954, suggesting that a visit to Washington by Andrew Hope and William Paul Sr. would be premature, noting that consideration of H.R. 1921 was postponed because of revisions made to the legislation by the Department of the Interior. It appears that Peterson and other advocates for Alaska Natives were taken by surprise by Interior's proposed revisions.

William "Bill" Paul Jr. at an ANB convention in the late 1940s. He provided a crucial service as grand secretary by bringing clarity to often-convoluted issues—like the rapidly mutating extinguishment legislation. Photo courtesy of Sealaska Heritage Institute, William Paul Jr. collection.

Peterson reported to Peratrovich and Hope the substance of the testimony NCAI representatives had made on behalf of the ANB to postpone congressional action on the bill. One legislator "tried to say that after all, you folks [the ANB] had had seven months in which to study the proposed revisions. At that point Congressman Aspinall of Colorado called his attention to the fact that you could not possibly have studied the January 11 proposed revisions [introduced only eleven days earlier]."

Peterson informed Mrs. Peratrovich that a colleague from the American Association on Indian Affairs "indicated he was going to advise Mr. Paul that, as far as he was concerned, [William Paul Sr. and Andrew Percy Hope] were not the spokesmen for the ANB on the bill." Helen Peterson, demonstrating her appreciation for who was in charge, wrote that she would not allow her colleagues to dictate to the ANB: "as far as the NCAI is concerned, we get our instructions from our authorized field representative, Mrs. Elizabeth Peratrovich, and the secretary of the ANB, Mr. John Hope."[173]

To resolve the question of representation of the ANB in Washington, D.C., John Hope sought direction from Grand Camp President Patrick Paul (no relation to William Paul). The president responded on February 6, 1954, with a maddeningly indirect letter. Instead of answering Hope's query directly, President Paul deferred to a letter he attached from ANB executive committeeman Alfred Widmark, who had advised President Paul against sending William Paul Sr. to Washington. Widmark's reasoning was the ANB should not be underwriting Paul's *Tee-Hit-Ton* case, which Widmark characterized as a private interest lawsuit.[174]

Although William Paul was being shunted aside, it was his aggressive pursuit of the *Tee-Hit-Ton* lawsuit that may have saved aboriginal title from being rendered irrelevant. The decision on *Tee-Hit-Ton*, issued by the Court of Claims in April 1954, found that neither the Treaty of Cession nor any subsequent act of Congress had "recognized" Alaska aboriginal title. The court also found that "unrecognized title" was not private property. Therefore, the Takings Clause of the Fifth Amendment did not apply and, consequently, "the Tee-Hit-Tons were not entitled to payment for their loss."[175]

James Peacock, representing the clan, appealed *Tee-Hit-Ton* to the U.S. Supreme Court, which agreed on June 7, 1954, to review the case. Considering the Supreme Court's impending review of aboriginal title in the *Tee-Hit-Ton* case, the Department of the Interior's legislative counsel advised Congress to take no further action on H.R. 1921, apparently expecting a favorable decision from the U.S. Supreme Court that would eliminate the need to enact the legislation. "[With] Bob Bartlett's wholehearted agreement, the subcommittee members voted to stop work on H.R. 1921."[176] According to Mitchell, had the revised version been enacted, "Alaska Natives would have been left with no money and little land other than the few acres located inside the [boundaries] of their villages."[177]

Concurrently, another attempt was in the works to deny aboriginal claims: Senator Butler, R-Montana, who did not believe aboriginal title existed in Alaska, pushed forward amendments to the Alaska statehood bill that included a "disclaimer clause" in name only. The clause Butler proposed would have achieved the intent of the revisions to H.R. 1921 made by the Departments of Interior and Justice limiting Native claims to land "in the possession and actually in the use or occupation of [Alaska Natives]...or any community of such Natives." The statehood bill was now worded to allow the State of Alaska to select any "vacant, unappropriated and unreserved" land other than the few acres of "real property that is owned by or, for a period of at least three years immediately prior to the enactment of this act, has been in the possession and actually in the use or occupation of [Alaska Natives]." In other words, Natives would receive the property they occupied within the boundaries of their villages but little more.[178]

This statehood legislation died when the House of Representatives failed to pass the Hawaii-Alaska statehood bill. So did Senator Butler, who passed away in his sleep in July of 1954 at the age of seventy-six.

Thus ended the most serious of the legislative threats to aboriginal title in Alaska. Although the Supreme Court upheld the lower court's *Tee-Hit-Ton* ruling, issuing its decision in February 1955, it conceded that aboriginal title existed—that such title remained as yet unextinguished. The decision was a severe personal loss for William Paul, the Tee-Hit-Ton clan, and the lawyers representing them, but the silver lining for Alaska Natives was the court's conclusion that aboriginal title in fact existed and, other than for specified lands, such title had not been extinguished by Congress. The *Tee-Hit-Ton* decision cast a legal cloud over vast tracts of Alaska.

The statehood bill was resurrected in January 1955 as S. 49. With Democrats back in control of Congress, Bob Bartlett succeeded in restoring the disclaimer clause that became Section 4 of the Alaska Statehood Act.[179] Under this clause, future citizens of Alaska disavowed "all right and title...to any lands or other property (including fishing rights), the right or title to which may be held by any Indians, Eskimos, or Aleuts (hereinafter called Natives)...or is held by the U.S. in trust for said natives."[180] With a disclaimer clause neutral on the topic of aboriginal rights, the issue was left to be resolved at a future date.

ANB leaders circa 1965. Back row, from left: Roy Peratrovich, Andrew P. Hope, Cyril Zuboff, Elizabeth (Mrs. Joe) Williams, Al Widmark, Mark Jacobs Sr., John Hope. Front row, from left: Frank Peratrovich, Joe Williams, Steve Hotch, Percy Hope, Cyrus Peck Sr. Photo courtesy of the Alaska State Historical Library.

The Alaska Constitutional Convention, which took place in Fairbanks from November 6, 1955, to February 6, 1956, brought together fifty-five elected delegates from throughout Alaska, among them Frank Peratrovich, the only Alaska Native who participated in drafting Alaska's constitution. In April of 1956, in a special referendum, Alaskans ratified the constitution, which included a disclaimer clause similar to that of S. 49, by a two-thirds vote of approval.

Two years later the U.S. House of Representatives passed the Alaska Statehood Act by a vote of 208 to 166, and the Senate by 64 to 20. President Eisenhower signed the bill into law on July 7, 1958.

In 1959, the U.S. Court of Claims decided the *Tlingit and Haida* case by finding that Alaska Natives did indeed have uncompensated claims to lands and resources since aboriginal title had yet to be extinguished by the U.S. government.

Paying no attention to potential Native claims, and heedless of Section 4 of the Alaska Statehood Act, officials of the new State of Alaska proceeded with oil lease sales and land selections that began to alarm Native leaders. The subsequent Native protests created, according to Stephen Haycox, "a huge conundrum, for doubts about title inhibited potential investors from taking any action toward development until they could be assured there would be no title questions."[181]

In January 1966, a twenty-two-year-old Inupiat, Charlie Edwardsen Jr. of Barrow, wrote to William Paul Sr.[182] In his letter, Edwardsen informed Paul that he and other Inupiaq were in the process of organizing the North Slope Native Association. They were organizing, he wrote, because their ancestral lands were "being exploited for oil and other minerals by the state and federal governments and also by private agencies....We want your advice and counsel in the matter and will want you to act as attorney for the group."[183]

Two weeks later, Paul wrote to the federal Bureau of Land Management and to Alaska Governor Bill Egan on behalf of his client, the North Slope Native Association, asserting aboriginal title to "the expanse of Alaska north of the Brooks Range, some sixty million acres of federal land."[184]

Paul's letter set in motion a series of events that led Secretary of the Interior Stewart Udall, in December 1966, to indefinitely suspend oil leases on the North Slope—the first step in what was to become a much broader "land freeze" that would not be lifted until the issue of aboriginal title in Alaska was settled.[185] In the face of intense pressure from the State of Alaska, Udall stood his ground, writing in a letter to Edgar Paul Boyko, then-Governor Wally Hickel's attorney general, on August 10, 1967: "This is a highly complex legal, political and moral problem. I trust the state is not intent upon depriving the Alaska Natives of the lands they use and occupy and need for their livelihood."[186]

With the land freeze, in part a consequence of Paul's letter, the State of Alaska was checked and forced to find a way out of the position. By virtue of his longevity and persistence, William Paul Sr., who had helped initiate the Alaska Native claims movement in 1929, played a key role in the final resolution of those claims.

In 1968, the year Alaska sold nearly a billion dollars' worth of oil leases to the North Slope, the effort to settle Alaska Native claims began to gather momentum. Here, Alaska Sen. Ernest Gruening and Washington Sen. Henry "Scoop" Jackson (second and third from left) meet with AFN representatives, from left, Laura Bergt, John Borbridge Jr., and, lower level, Willie Hensley, Don Wright, Emil Notti, and Flore Lekanof. Photo courtesy of John Borbridge Jr.

8

Shaping Alaska

In the first half of the twentieth century, no other organization in Alaska was capable, as the ANB proved to be, of legitimizing Alaska Native aspirations, winning basic rights, and protecting aboriginal claims.

With its national allies, the Alaska Native Brotherhood was not alone, but it was indispensable. Without it, Alaska's congressional delegates would have had no credible organization with which to collaborate on issues of importance to Alaska Natives, and without the ANB all those who represented Alaska Native interests before Congress would have been without credentials.

Under the circumstances that played out in the early 1950s, can credit be fairly given to the ANB for saving Alaska Native claims? If one considers the likely course of events without the influence of the ANB during consideration of the several extinguishment bills, most especially H.R. 1921, then yes, credit must be given. While the ANB had only a small role in blocking statehood legislation that included Senator Butler's claims-killing amendment to the disclaimer clause, no basketball game has ever been won through fortuitous circumstances by a team that was not on the court. And in this game, the ANB was the only Alaska Native organization playing defense.[187]

Ironically, Southeast Alaska Natives were nearly excluded from the statewide movement to settle Alaska Native claims. The leaders representing the Inupiaq, Yup'ik, Athabascan, and Aleut groups who in 1966 founded the Alaska Federation of Natives (AFN) did not invite the Natives of Southeast to join their organization. According to Emil Notti, an Athabascan leader who served as the organization's first president, the reasoning was that the

Tlingit and Haida people had already "won" their Court of Claims lawsuit in 1959. But in January of 1968 the paltry nature of the victory became all too apparent when the U.S. Court of Claims awarded the Central Council of Tlingit and Haida Tribes of Alaska a mere $7.5 million judgment award, an amount based on the ostensible value in the early 1900s of the only commodity the court recognized: "merchantable timber."[188] Sentiments within the AFN changed just enough so that the organization agreed, by the narrowest of margins (Notti's tie-breaking vote), to include the Native people of Southeast Alaska in the statewide effort to settle Alaska Native claims.[189]

It soon became apparent that the AFN had made a wise decision. Using the interest earnings of the settlement fund, the Central Council, led by John Borbridge Jr., established offices, hired staff, and began working in concert with the AFN in the national effort to reach a settlement. To overstate the skills that veterans of the Alaska Native Brotherhood brought to the AFN might offend other Alaska Natives, but few would deny that the men and women of the ANB/ANS were experts in organizational procedures. In the words of Emil Notti himself, "The best parliamentarians came out of the ANB—they knew how to organize."[190]

Crucially, in early 1971, the Central Council, an organization founded by the ANB, loaned the AFN $100,000 to support the final congressional lobbying effort, in which Borbridge played an important role.[191]

With the State of Alaska frozen out of land selections and with the discovery of a massive oil field at Prudhoe Bay, the cloud hanging over the title to Alaska lands had to be removed. These circumstances conspired with new attitudes toward civil rights and equal justice to result in the largest resolution of aboriginal claims in the history of the United States—the Alaska Native Claims Settlement Act, which was signed into law on December 18, 1971.

It had taken the United States more than one hundred years to recognize that the 1867 Treaty of Cession with the Russians had left aboriginal title unresolved and that the people who used and occupied the land surrounding the isolated Russian outposts were the original owners of Alaska.

ANCSA has served to vindicate early ANB leaders who believed so strongly in American ideals, among the most important of which is chiseled above the entrance to the U.S. Supreme Court: Equal Justice Under

Law. The men and women who initiated the Alaska Native claims movement at the 1929 Grand Camp convention in Haines were under no illusion that an ideal such as equal justice could be easily achieved, especially at a time when Natives could claim few privileges of citizenship. Educated Alaska Natives in the early twentieth century were well aware of the government's history of injustice and broken promises to Native Americans and of the crude discrimination of a society that did not recognize their equal rights until 1945.

Whether Alaska Natives could have done better than the Alaska Native Claims Settlement Act will be debated far into the future. But from the standpoint of the ANB, the organization's long-sought goals—unrestricted title to land, fair compensation, and self-determination—were achieved.

Few characteristics are more prominent among the Northwest Coast cultures than the belief that honor demands that debts be paid, and that in such matters time is immaterial. Although many of the men and women who led the ANB and ANS set aside traditions and mastered English to achieve their goals, their cultural inheritance drove them to persist through more than four decades, from 1929 to 1971, to ensure that the debt owed to their people was honored.

The confidence and determination of a host of Alaska Natives, many more than the people mentioned in these pages, made the American ideal of equal justice under law more than an abstraction. Whatever else might be said about the Alaska Native Claims Settlement Act, there would have been little left to settle had the ANB not deployed the sword and the shield by which they defined, then protected Alaska Native claims. It is to all those who attended the meetings, contributed their dues, raised funds, and engaged in the debates of the ANB/ANS Grand Camp conventions that all Alaskans owe a debt of gratitude for shaping the State of Alaska as we know it today.

Notes

Introduction

1. Haycox, *Alaska: An American Colony*, 237.
2. The Alaska Native Brotherhood and the Alaska Native Sisterhood are distinct organizations, but they act in concert during their annual joint Grand Camp meetings. Because our research discovered little evidence of the Sisterhood's direct involvement in the political or legal issues surrounding aboriginal claims, we refer throughout to the ANB.

    There is some uncertainty as to when, exactly, the Alaska Native Sisterhood was organized—1915 is a consensus date for the start of the predecessor organizations that coalesced as the Alaska Native Sisterhood at the 1926 Grand Camp Convention in Klukwan. The Alaska Native Sisterhood was recognized as a formal auxiliary of the Alaska Native Brotherhood in 1927, at which time its members became full voting participants in the Grand Camp conventions.

    For a description of the working relationship between the ANB and ANS, see Walter Soboleff's comments in caption on page 22, excerpted from Kim Metcalfe, *In Sisterhood*, 13–14.
3. Alaska's congressional delegation—Ted Stevens (R) and Mike Gravel (D) in the Senate and Alaska's sole member of the House, Don Young (R)— were implacable in their opposition to ANILCA, which they viewed as an effort by national environmental organizations to "lock up" Alaska's resources. Demonstrating the nonpartisan nature of their opposition, Senator Gravel succeeded in temporarily derailing ANILCA in 1978, although he had insufficient influence to kill it.

    In 1980, everyone associated with the legislation knew that with Ronald Reagan as president, Alaska's delegation, now all Republican with the election of Frank Murkowski to the Senate, could kill or severely restrict ANILCA. Consequently, President Carter signed the bill, flaws and all, into law on December 2, 1980, before Reagan took office.

    During subsequent presidential administrations, Alaska's delegation, aided by the congressional seniority system, got stronger and almost certainly would have stopped any legislation similar in scale to ANILCA.
4. Although the legislation extinguished aboriginal rights to fish and game, promises were extracted from congressional leaders, who returned to the

issue in ANILCA, by which subsistence rights were extended to all rural Alaskans. Subsistence remains an unsettled issue because the State of Alaska refused to comply with the federal law, thus leading to federal reassertion of fish and game management on federal land and waters in Alaska.

5.   The U.S. Constitution (Article I, Section 8) delegates to Congress responsibility for making laws with respect to Native Americans. On some matters concerning tribes, Congress has at times deferred to tribal consent, but there was no legal requirement nor political pressure to put the Alaska Native claims settlement of 1971 to an Alaska Native referendum (a criticism common among recent generations of Alaska Natives). Considering the absence of federally recognized tribes in Alaska at that time and the lack of any means to verify who among the citizens of Alaska were actually Alaska Natives, such a vote would have been a practical impossibility.

The perception lingers that the Alaska Federation of Natives could have rejected the ANCSA settlement they had a hand in negotiating, but in reality, when the organization voted to approve the legislation, the bill had already been signed into law. See Mitchell, *Take My Land, Take My Life*, 491–493.

6.   In addition to the twelve regional corporations, many Alaska Natives who were living outside of Alaska at the time became shareholders of the 13th Regional Corporation. The corporation, headquartered in Seattle, received no land and does not receive distributions as do other regional corporations from the profit redistribution requirement of ANCSA, known as Section 7(i), and has suffered serious business setbacks, including a period of bankruptcy.

An often-overlooked aspect of ANCSA is that it transferred forty-four million acres of federal land in Alaska to state-chartered corporations. So, in addition to the approximately 104 million acres the State of Alaska was entitled to receive under the terms of the Alaska Statehood Act, another forty-four million acres of Native-owned private property came under state jurisdiction courtesy of ANCSA. Lands conveyed to Alaska Native corporations under the terms of ANCSA are subject to the same state and municipal laws as any privately owned land in Alaska—including zoning, building codes, criminal matters, fish and wildlife, and so on. Congressional amendments subsequent to ANCSA (the so-called 1991 amendments) now protect undeveloped ANCSA land from local or state taxation, but if an Alaska Native corporation develops land conveyed under the terms of ANCSA, then that land becomes subject to existing tax laws.

7.   The relative growth of Alaska Natives' political influence following ANCSA can be measured by two well-documented accomplishments: the lobbying effort that began in the mid-1980s to amend ANCSA and the 2010 general election write-in campaign to reelect Lisa Murkowski as U.S. senator. Both

efforts were led by the Alaska Federation of Natives with significant contributions, financial and otherwise, from Alaska Native corporations.

The 1991 amendments, which were enacted in February 1988, neutralized the deadline of December 18, 1991, when ANCSA shares were to become "alienable" (could be sold). Other aspects of the amendments altered the nature of ANCSA by adding elements strongly valued by Alaska Natives (such as allowing Alaska Native corporations to enroll children who were born after ANCSA became law and special benefits for elder shareholders), all of which made Alaska Native corporations unique among American for-profit corporations. Although Alaska Natives were participants in the effort to pass ANCSA, it is generally conceded that other forces, principally oil interests, were compelling a settlement. With the 1991 amendments, Alaska Natives were the motive force.

In 2010, Alaska Natives were again the motive force, this time in a political battle during the Alaska general election campaign for U.S. senator. In a major upset, Joe Miller, a Tea Party candidate, beat incumbent Senator Lisa Murkowski in the Republican primary. During the primary campaign, Miller had made statements that Alaska Natives found offensive and some they found threatening to Alaska Native corporation business interests. With strong encouragement from Alaska Native leaders, Murkowski chose to enter the general election as an independent write-in candidate. Alaska Native corporations rallied behind Murkowski and made generous donations (at least $1.7 million, or roughly 44 percent of the total funds raised) to a political action committee dedicated to her reelection. During its October 2010 convention, the Alaska Federation of Natives voted by acclamation to back the Murkowski write-in campaign and then provided strong get-out-the-vote support in the final days of the election. Of the 258,746 votes cast, Miller received 90,839 (35 percent) of the total while his Democratic challenger, Scott McAdams, garnered 60,045 (23 percent), but an unprecedented 102,234 (40 percent) of the votes were cast as write-in, 99 percent of which were directed to Murkowski's reelection. Rural districts, with Alaska Natives in strong majorities, provided the highest per-capita percentages of write-in votes. After a series of challenges by Joe Miller's campaign, the election was finally certified on December 28, 2010, and Lisa Murkowski was reelected to the U.S. Senate, beating Miller by 10,252 votes. Since then, Murkowski has readily acknowledged in public statements that without the strong support of Alaska Natives she could not have won reelection. (Information about the Murkowski write-in campaign can be found through searches of adn.com, website of the *Anchorage Daily News*; also see www. elections.alaska.gov.)

8.   *Tee-Hit-Ton Indians v. United States*, 120 F.Supp. 202, 128 Ct. Cl. 82 (legal citation for the decision in the Court of Claims in 1954); 348 U.S. 272,

75 S.Ct. 313, 99 L.Ed. 314, reh. denied, 348 U.S. 965, 75 S.Ct. 521, 99 L.Ed. 753 (1955) (legal citation for the decision of the U.S. Supreme Court, issued February 7, 1955). See http://supreme.justia.com/us/348/272/case.html.

   Tlingit and Haida Indians of Alaska v. United States, 177 F. Supp. 452, 147 Ct. Cl. 315 (legal citation for the decision of the Court of Claims issued Oct. 7, 1959, which held that the Tlingit and Haida people "as a tribe, had established aboriginal Indian title...by their exclusive use and occupancy of that territory from time immemorial"; and 389 F. 2d 778 (legal citation for the Court of Claims decision, on January 19, 1968, setting the amount of the recovery award for lands taken). See http://openjurist. org/389/f2d/778.

Chapter One

9.   In *Alaska Natives and American Laws* (2002), Case and Voluck demonstrate the validity of aboriginal title in Alaska. However, even after *Tlingit and Haida Indians of Alaska v. United States*, aboriginal title to land remained unsettled until the Alaska Native Claims Settlement Act extinguished aboriginal claims in exchange for money and specific tracts of lands. As Case and Voluck conclude, other Native claims, particularly rights to fish and game, remain unsettled to this day. Case and Voluck, 35–63.

10.   The legal and political status of Indian tribes was established by the U.S. Supreme Court decisions in *Johnson v. M'Intosh* (1823), *Cherokee Nation v. Georgia* (1831), and *Worcester v. Georgia* (1832). These are known as the Marshall Trilogy in reference to Chief Justice John Marshall, who served from 1801 until his death in 1835 at the age of seventy-nine.

   Johnson v. M'intosh, 21 U.S. 543 (1823), http://supreme.justia.com/ cases/federal/us/21/543/case.html; *Cherokee Nation v. Georgia*, 30 U.S. 1 (1831), http://supreme.justia.com/cases/federal/us/30/1/case.html; *Worcester v. Georgia*, 31 U.S. 515 (1832); http://supreme.justia.com/cases-es/federal/us/31/515/case.html.

11.   Mitchell, *Sold American*, 262.

12.   Langdon, "Honoring Our Founders," a speech delivered on October 2, 2012, at the hundredth-anniversary ANB Grand Camp convention. In *The Fishermen's Frontier* (67), David Arnold cites other examples of commercial fishing interests averting conflict by recognizing Indian rights to salmon streams and paying for fishing privileges. Which is not to say that the region was free of any conflict. At least twice, the broadsides of U.S. Navy vessels obliterated Tlingit villages: three in the Kake area in 1869 and Angoon in 1882.

13.   Arnold, 94.

14.   Mackovjak, *Alaska Salmon Traps*, 12.

15.   Ibid., 14.

16.   Arnold, 72.

17 Ibid., 63.
18. Ibid., 94.
19. Mitchell, *Sold American*, 262.
20. Personal communication with Stephen Langdon, April 22, 2010.
21. Arnold, 66.
22. Wallace M. Olson, professor of anthropology (emeritus), University of Alaska Southeast, has studied the early European exploration of Alaska extensively and has published several books on the subject. In an email response after reviewing an early manuscript of this book, he elaborated on the European practice of taking "possession" of land:

> The common assumption by Europeans in the 18th century [was based on] "terra nullius." The Latin term literally means, "land owned by no one." The concept was that these 'undiscovered lands' could be claimed by European powers, unless another European power had previously claimed them by some "act of possession." That is, that indigenous people were incapable of being "owners" of their lands since they were...somehow inferior.

Olson noted that the Europeans maintained this philosophy despite encounters with many Native societies, particularly of Central and South America, that had "developed huge empires and produced monumental works, had evolved writing systems and had a knowledge of astronomy and mathematics."

Arnold (p. 14) addressed the topic of how the expropriation of Native resources was justified by Euro-Americans:

> Since the time of European contact, Native American history and identity have been bound up with caricatures—the "idle savage," the "barbarian savage," the "noble savage." Each stereotype expressed more about Euro-Americans than it did about Natives Americans. The "idle savage" portrayed Indian peoples as lazy and undeserving of the vast "wild" territories that surrounded their villages. To a people like the English, who believed that land ownership carried with it the legal and moral responsibility of "improvement"..."idle" Indians therefore had no legitimate claim to the land. The ruthless and heathen character of the "barbarian savage" justified the military dispossession of his lands. Even the more romantic notion of the "noble savage," which associated primitiveness with virtue, was used by Euro-Americans for their own purposes to critique modern society and, in the twentieth century, to promote conservation and environmental concerns.

23. The Treaty of Cession, Article III:

> The inhabitants of the ceded territory, according to their choice, reserving their natural allegiance, may return to Russia within

three years; but if they should prefer to remain in the ceded territory, they, with the exception of uncivilized native tribes, shall be
admitted to the enjoyment of all the rights, advantages, and immunities of citizens of the United States, and shall be maintained
and protected in the free enjoyment of their liberty, property, and
religion. The uncivilized tribes will be subject to such laws and
regulations as the United States may, from time to time, adopt in
regard to aboriginal tribes of that country.

Article III was written such that it appeared to consider that some
Natives, who had been treated as "civilized" by the Russians, were entitled
to share in the same "rights, advantages, and immunities" of U.S. citizens.
Determining who was civilized and who was not would occupy civil au-
thorities in Alaska for decades to come.

24. Case and Voluck, 44–49.
25. In 1924, Congress passed the Indian Citizenship Act (also known as the
Snyder Act). Although the Fourteenth Amendment, passed just after the
end of the Civil War, granted citizenship to all persons born in the United
States, it only applied to those "subject to the jurisdiction" of the United
States. Indians, who were considered members of sovereign tribes, were not
subject to U.S. jurisdiction and therefore not eligible for citizenship through
the Fourteenth Amendment. By 1924, many Native Americans had become
citizens through other means, but the 1924 act resolved all questions of citizenship for Alaska Natives, and henceforth they were able to vote. But that
was half the battle: it was not until the Anti-Discrimination Act of 1945
that the civil rights of Alaska Natives received equal protection under the
laws of Alaska. While the questions of citizenship and equal protection had
been settled, whether or not U.S. Indian policy applied to Alaska Natives
remained unsettled and not seriously addressed until after the Indian Self-
Determination and Education Assistance Act became law in 1975.
26. "[Indian title] is not a property right but amounts to a right of occupancy,
which the sovereign grants and protects against intrusion by third parties,"
Tee-Hit-Ton 348 U.S. 272, 279 (1955).
27. The Court of Claims held in *Tlingit and Haida Indians of Alaska v. United
States,* on October 7, 1959, that the Tlingit and Haida people "as a tribe, had
established aboriginal Indian title ... by their exclusive use and occupancy
of that territory from time immemorial" (177 F. Supp. 452, 147 Ct. Cl. 315).

According to the declarations of facts made in the 1968 decision, "Our
1959 decision developed the factual background of this case in detail and
only a brief review of the development of this litigation is appropriate.
It involves valuing six separate areas of over 17,500,000 acres, each area
having a different valuation date ranging from 1891 to 1925, different re-

sources, and numerous land parcels patented over a 50-year period" (389 F. 2d 778, Ct. Cl 1968).

The statement of facts admitted that the U.S. government had taken 85,730 acres by establishing the Annette Island reservation, 14,956,312 acres by executive proclamations to establish the Tongass National Forest, and 2,558,246 acres to be set aside for the Glacier Bay National Monument. The court found that some 2,634,744 acres, most of which were scattered along the mountainous boundary with Canada, had not been included in any taking. Since title to these remnants was not subject to the court's ruling, Southeast Alaska Natives had another rationale for being included in the Alaska Native Claims Settlement Act.

As Robert Price writes in *The Great Father in Alaska*, the U.S. Court of Claims appointed a commissioner to determine a compensable amount. In 1966, the commissioner recommended $15,909,368. "This amount was reduced by about half when the Court of Claims rejected any compensation for the fishery property claim," writes Price. "Of course, this was the main economic loss suffered by the Tlingit and Haida, and was the main reason for requesting Congress to pass a jurisdictional act" (p. 100).

The award decision ignored any values related to fisheries, gold mining, or logging on the lands after the time of taking from the Tlingit and Haida people by the federal government.

The tortured nature of the award ruling is captured by the dissenting judge, Philip Nichols Jr., who wrote:

No doubt…as the court says, no one owns or can own any exclusive fishing rights in navigable water, other than, perhaps, relating to shellfish.…I would have supposed that one who owned as plaintiffs here did, all the vast lands bordering on so many sounds, bays, and coves, teeming with fish, would have enjoyed such enormous advantages over others in exploiting the fisheries thereon that willing buyers would have paid enhanced prices for the land, even if they could obtain therewith no ownership in the fish. A person owning a building on Fifth Avenue might claim it was worth more because of its favorable location without thereby asserting any proprietorship in the vehicular and pedestrian traffic daily passing by his door.

For the court's 1968 ruling, see: http://openjurist.org/389/f2d/778/tlingit-and-haida-indians-of-alaska-v-united-states.

28. The Alaska Native claims movement of the early 1960s lies outside the scope of this book. A close reading of that period reveals that the idea of significant land conveyances to Alaska Natives was highly unpopular in Congress (Mitchell, *Take My Land, Take My Life*, 112).

29. The organization was officially renamed the Central Council of Tlingit and Haida Indian Tribes of Alaska after legislation passed by Congress in 1965 authorized the Central Council to receive the award settlement of the *Tlingit and Haida Indians v. United States* lawsuit.

Chapter Two

30. In his self-published history *The Emergence of Tlingit Christianity* (p. 300), Dr. Joseph Bettridge, a Presbyterian minister, quoted C. F. Jones, pastor of the Presbyterian Church in Juneau, as being well acquainted with "the Tlingits' legal status in the newly organized territory, noting Jones's perception of the unjust political status of Native people circa 1914: "A Tlingit can acquire no title to anything: land, homestead or any other property. He is declared not a citizen of any country. Since he supports himself, he is not a ward of any country, and yet the United States claims to have jurisdiction over him. It sues him but will not let him vote. In rights he is treated as a foreigner but in punishment as a citizen."

31. The ANB founders were George Field, William Hobson, James C. Johnson, Eli Katanook, Seward Kunz, Paul Liberty, Frank Mercer, Marie Orsen, Frank Price, Peter Simpson, James Watson, Chester Worthington, and Ralph Young. See Dauenhauer and Dauenhauer, *Haa Kusteeyí, Our Culture*, 619–695.

32. Ibid., 648.

33. Ibid. Building the first ANB hall was a formative experience that weakened the affiliation between the ANB and the Presbyterian Church (see Note 50).

34. In the decades before statehood, the campaign to suppress indigenous languages by the educational system, secular and religious, is remembered as particularly abusive. There is no denying the intense hostility of the dominant culture in those days to Alaska Native cultures, languages, and lifestyles. Handed down from one generation to the next are stories of teachers who resorted to mouth washing, switching, ruler whacking, and racial humiliation when their young Native charges spoke their first language, but other forces were also at work. Among the strongest influences were economic. During the Russian era in Alaska, Native cultural traditions and languages remained largely unchanged, likely due to the market relationship with indigenous suppliers that put the Russians at a disadvantage. Isolated in their Southeast Alaska enclaves, the Russians of the early 1800s found themselves at the ends of the earth, so far removed from their base of supplies in western Russia that they depended on Tlingits and Haidas for much of their food and a large share of furs (the raison d'être of the Russian colony). The Russians also found themselves in competition with English and American traders who offered better and cheaper goods of the type strongly favored by Natives. The Russians provided few employment opportuni-

ties, and with their status more often that of needy customer, there was no compelling reason for the Natives of Southeast Alaska to learn Russian or conform to Russian traditions. As Americans took control of the region in the last quarter of the nineteenth century, commercial fishing, seafood processing, and mining operations were established. Natives quickly learned that those who spoke English tended to get the best jobs and were the most successful at establishing commercial relationships with Americans, who showed little tolerance for or interest in learning other languages. As Sergei Kan explains, the Russian missions that remained after the sale of Russian holdings in Alaska had increasing difficulties sustaining their relevance among the Native people, in part because Native parents were disappointed that the priests did not teach their children how to speak "Bostonian." In this context, the desire by Native parents for their children to learn English can be viewed as a practical accommodation to the by-then dominant culture. See Kan, *A Russian American Photographer in Tlingit Country*, 39; see also Dauenhauers, *Haa Kusteeyí, Our Culture*, 71.

35. "Native Culture Resolution of the Alaska Presbytery," October 21, 1991, which stated in part: "We disavow those teachings which led people to believe that abandoning native culture was a prerequisite for being Christian. We deeply regret the church's part in the destruction of native artifacts and the church's part in the loss of native languages" (www.presbofak. org/Portals/presbofak/Native%20Culture%20Resolution%20of%20 AK%20Pres.pdf).

36. In his unpublished manuscript, "The History of the Alaska Native Brotherhood," the late John Hope wrote:

> One of the more important actions taken by the delegates to [the 1939 Grand Camp] convention was the adoption of Resolution 37, which designated the Executive Committee of the ANB as the "Central Council of the [Tlingit] and Haida Land Suit" (a.k.a, the "Tlingit-Haida Claims Committee"). A note worthy of mention is that Peter Simpson [a Tsimpshian], who was neither Tlingit nor Haida, was a member of that Executive Committee [that passed the resolution]. Indeed he was the "Father" of the Native Claims movement and it was natural that he be a part of the organization. (Andy Hope collection).

Peter Simpson is remembered for his fervent belief that Alaska Natives were deserving of full and equal citizenship. In the introduction to a 1911 editorial that Simpson wrote for *The Tlingit*, a newspaper produced at Sheldon Jackson School, he instructed the editor, George Beck, also the school's associate superintendent, to "print it just the way I write it." Simpson wrote the editorial, he explained, in hopes of "discouraging the old Indian life and encouraging new, noble, Christlife [*sic*] to our people."

He closed the brief introduction with these words: "This movement is just commencing and will go on until we win." As he made clear in the editorial that followed, titled "As an Alaskan Sees It," full and equal citizenship was the goal. While the editorial included a few grammatical quirks, it is an articulate and forceful renunciation of Alaska Native traditions as impediments to the attainment of civil liberties.

Such opinions were without question influenced by the assimilationist doctrines promoted by the Presbyterian Church, but to put the responsibility for such opinions on others ignores the self-motivation that characterized the early ANB leaders. These were men living stable lives, providing for their families, contributing to their communities, and taking firm stands in the face of substantial opposition—and often hate-fueled derision—on the social and political issues of the day.

Within a year of writing the editorial, Simpson, eleven other men, and one woman organized the Alaska Native Brotherhood. As the preamble to the ANB Constitution proclaims, they were inspired by the goal of advancing Alaska Natives so they might take their place "among the cultivated races of the world."

37. Ishmael Hope, "They Won't Be Forgotten," February 18, 2012.

38. The first recorded contact with Tlingits was on July 18, 1741, when Captain Chirikov, who commanded the *St. Paul* of the Bering Expedition, sent two boats to shore, believed to be somewhere north of Sitka, to refill water casks. While waiting for his crewmen to return, Chirikov reported seeing occupied canoes pass along the shore, but for reasons unknown, neither of the *St. Paul*'s boats returned. Three decades later, the Spanish began a series of expeditions to the Northwest Coast. The first, commanded by Juan José Pérez Hernández, made contact with the Haidas on the Queen Charolette Islands. Over the next decade, several more Spanish expeditions ventured into Tlingit country, by which time English and American explorations and trading expeditions had become common (see Olson, *Through Spanish Eyes*). For population estimates, see Hinkley, *The Canoe Rocks*, 18, n. 9; de Laguna, *The Tlingit Indian*, 20 and appendix; Langdon, *The Native People of Alaska*, 72 (3rd ed., 1993).

39. Vern Metcalfe. Interview with John Hope for *ANB History*. Produced and first aired by KTOO-FM Juneau in 1986. The cultural accommodation of Alaska Natives of Southeast Alaska is a fraught topic, and one deserving of new scholarship, especially by younger generations of well-educated Alaska Natives.

While there are few people now alive who are fluent in the Tlingit or Haida languages, many people are actively working on acquiring skills in these languages, either on their own or by participating in programs offered in schools and by Alaska Native heritage institutions.

The ceremonial gathering often called potlatch but more accurately referred to as *koo.èex* is central to the Pacific Northwest Coast cultures. The so-called Last Great Potlatch of 1904, hosted in Sitka, now seems an elaborate hoax to assuage missionaries who obviously imagined the event to be the last potlatch, great or otherwise. Judging from photographs of *koo.èex* and other activities that followed the Last Great Potlatch, Tlingit cultural practices were hiding in plain sight all along and continue to the present day.

40. Ishmael Hope, son of the late Andrew Hope III, is a researcher with Sealaska Heritage Institute. His blog, alaskanativestoryteller.com, is a source of contemporary Native views.

41. Personal communication, November 21, 2013.

42. Hope, http://alaskanativestoryteller.com/2012/02/they-wont-be-forgotten-the-leaders-of-the-alaska-native-brotherhood-and-sisterhood.

43. Steve Langdon, "Shakan Was Not Abandoned! Compulsory Education and the Forced Relocation of Tlingit Populations in the 20th Century," presentation made on March 27, 2009, at the Sharing Our Knowledge conference. (See http://clanconference.org.)

44. One of the best-documented examples of an ANB leader who refused to abandoned his role as a traditional leader can be found in "Rudolph Walton: One Man's Journey Through Stormy Seas," the thesis written by Walton's granddaughter, Joyce Walton Shales, for her doctorate in education from the University of British Columbia in 1998. See page 176.

45. Ibid., 99.

46. Ibid., 154.

47. Ibid., 178

48. Ibid., 179.

49. The apparent success of ANB leaders like Walton in navigating the racial attitudes of the dominant culture early in the twentieth century should not be viewed as the general experience of Alaska Natives, who, from the early American era through the post–World War II years and beyond, were exposed to unrestrained racial and cultural contempt at all levels of white society. Natives were compelled to reject their indigenous culture and language yet were found unacceptable for membership in the dominant culture. The consequences of such a paradox find expression in modern statistics that chart the socioeconomic and health disparities between Alaska Native and white populations. See Peter Metcalfe, *Gumboot Determination*, 209. For confirming statistics, see www.nida.nih.gov and www.worldhealth.net, which show that present-day disease and behavioral health problems afflict Alaska Natives in far greater proportion than Caucasians.

50. The author spoke with Sitka photographer Martin Strand two months before Strand's death on August 14, 2008. Strand was born in 1935 and grew up in the Cottages, the neighborhood adjacent to the Sheldon Jackson School

campus built by and for Sheldon Jackson School graduates. He remembered the story of the provocation that led the ANB to build its first community hall, which effectively began the first camp, Sitka #1. He said that when the Presbyterians' general disapproval of modern dancing became a prohibition of Tlingits dancing at church functions, a determined Peter Simpson led a march through town to the Indian Village (The Ranche) and supervised the construction of a new hall, which became ANB Camp #1. John Hope tells a similar version of the same story in his unpublished manuscript of ANB history (Andy Hope collection).

51. Metcalfe, Vern. Interview with Judson Brown, for *ANB History*. Produced and first aired by KTOO-FM Juneau in 1986.

52. Tillie Paul Tamaree had three sons, Samuel, William, and Louis, each of whom she sent to the Lower Forty-eight to complete their educations. Of the three, Samuel did not return to Alaska, although he remained in contact with his family. Tillie married William Tamaree sometime before 1904 (Paul, *Then Fight for It*, 27–33).

53. Haycox, "Then Fight for It: William Lewis Paul and Alaska Native Land Claims."

54. Haycox, *Alaska: An American Colony*, 239.

55. To overcome the illiteracy of many Alaska Native voters, William Paul provided them with cardboard guides that fit over the ballots. Spaces were cut out by which voters could make their marks next to the names of favored candidates. "Neither organizing a bloc of voters nor supplying the cardboard guides was illegal, but critics objected to their use on moral and political grounds" (Haycox, 238–39).

56. Charles Webster Demmert, an Alaska Native from the Craig/Klawock area, testified at the Hannah hearings on September 19, 1944. In response to Judge Hannah's interrogatory, Demmert described how Alaska Natives made use of "every inch" of shoreline along the islands of west-central Southeast Alaska until they were forced off their trapping grounds by fox farmers. He told Judge Hannah about the experience of an Alaska Native trapper: "One trapping season, toward spring, he went back there [to Edwards Island in Port Beauclerc, an inlet of Kuiu Island]. He had his dogs with him. And when he got ashore a [fox farmer] came out and said, 'Take your dogs aboard or I am going to shoot them. Take your dogs aboard.' And [the trapper's] houses were right there. At that time he had two little houses. He had a smokehouse, and he had a house with a stove. He was ordered to take his children aboard, take his dogs aboard [and leave]. Demmert's story concluded with a description of how the trapper pursued restitution: "And the old man made a trip to Juneau to report to the court. He could not talk English. He made three or four trips to Juneau, and finally they paid him one hundred dollars, hush-

up money." See also: Paul, *Then Fight for It*, 81; Isto, *Fur Farms of Alaska*, 161–62; and Mitchell, *Sold American*, 259–61.

57.   William Paul's story, as recounted in Fred Paul's *Then Fight for It* (82), is disputed by Donald Craig Mitchell, who credits Judge James Wickersham for the idea of the Tlingit and Haida people suing the government (see *Sold American*, 262). Mitchell criticizes William Paul Sr. for claiming the idea was his. Mitchell is on firm ground in pointing out that suing the government was Wickersham's, not Paul's, idea. But this is arguing the wrong premise.

As Mitchell himself points out in *Sold American*, jurisdictional acts on behalf of Native Americans were fairly common: "on eight occasions during the twelve years Wickersham served as delegate, Congress enacted legislation that authorized an Indian tribe to sue the United States in the Court of Claims to obtain a money judgment for the value of land taken from its members." In other words, the idea of suing the government was hardly more remarkable than advising a client to pursue a class action lawsuit.

The only question here of historical significance involves who was responsible for starting the process that led to the Alaska Native Claims Settlement Act of 1971. That the land had been taken without payment was a commonplace grievance among Tlingits, first voiced by traditional leaders when Russia ceded Alaska to the United States in 1867. Stephen Langdon gave a speech at the 2012 ANB/ANS Grand Camp convention on the one hundredth anniversary of the ANB in which he shared with his audience some findings of his research into the interactions of American officials and Tlingits following the Treaty of Cession with Russia. Langdon told of a Tlingit leader, Chief Johnson, who, in 1869, "led a group of Tlingit leaders back to Washington, D.C., and in the political capital of the U.S., informed U.S. leaders that their claims were illegitimate and would not be recognized by the Tlingit leaders. The facts presented and objections were not acted upon but the Tlingit clearly stated their views" (Langdon, "Honoring Our Founders").

According to nineteenth-century historian Hubert Howe Bancroft (*History of Alaska*, 609):

> The discontent [of the Tlingit] arose, not from any antagonism to the Americans, but from the fact that the territory had been sold without their consent; and that they had received none of the proceeds of the sale. The Russians ... had been allowed to occupy the territory partly for mutual benefit, but their forefathers had dwelt in Alaska long before any white man had set foot in America. Why had not the seven and a half million dollars been paid to them instead of the Russians?

The ANB members of the 1920s knew they held the note for an unpaid debt owed to the Alaska Native people by the U.S. government, but at the time they were struggling to obtain the full rights of citizenship, and many apparently feared that suing the United States would risk the attainment of those rights.

According to William Paul's story, as Mitchell relates it, in 1926 Paul tried to convince the ANB Grand Camp to sue the government, but the delegates were incredulous, viewing Paul's idea as "a fantasy." Based on the interactions between Paul and Wickersham recorded in Wickersham's diaries, the two met in 1921. It seems entirely plausible that several years before the 1929 convention, Paul, fired up by the realization that the Native people of Southeast Alaska could file a suit against the United States, began discussing it with ANB leaders.

In 1929, William Paul was ANB Grand Camp president. Without Paul inviting Wickersham, then orchestrating the presentation to the ANB/ANS Grand Camp, and without Peter Simpson's behind-the-scenes support, the judge's proposal would most likely have been politely received and quietly ignored.

Although Paul was at the height of his influence with the ANB, it is doubtful that, even with Simpson's support, he could have talked the Grand Camp delegates into as bold an action as suing the government without the cover provided by someone of Wickersham's stature: a respected jurist and progressive politician known to be supportive of Native interests.

In 1929 Wickersham was seventy-two years old, and while he had a well-established reputation for being a friend of Alaska Natives, no indication can be found in his diaries that he had extensive relationships with individual Southeast Alaska Natives other than William Paul.

There can be little doubt that William Paul's role was crucial, first in convincing the ANB to follow Wickersham's advice and sue the government, then in keeping them on board through the lobbying effort that led to the passage of the Jurisdictional Act of 1935.

During these years, no one had greater influence within the ANB than Peter Simpson. Had he opposed suing the government, it is difficult to imagine the organization taking such action. His direct role is obscure, but according to John Hope's description, Simpson typically worked behind the scenes, urging younger men to take the lead.

Mitchell characterizes the description of the exchange between Simpson and Paul when Simpson "whispered" in Paul's ear, and Paul's assertion that suing the government had been his plan for several years prior to 1929, as Paul's "self-promoting prevarication." This seems a bit harsh: that Wickersham's suggestion had become Paul's plan hardly qualifies as an evasion of the truth.

To be fair, it would appear that Wickersham, Paul, and Simpson all deserve their share of credit, but Paul was pivotal. One certainty is that in 1929, the Alaska Native Brotherhood and the Alaska Native Sisterhood meeting in Grand Camp convention at Haines started the Alaska Native claims movement by their vote to sue the government.

58. Vern Metcalfe interview with John Hope.

59. Mitchell, *Sold American*, 231.

60. Vern Metcalfe interview with Judson Brown.

61. James Wickersham's diaries can be downloaded from the Alaska State Library's website and then searched for key words. No entry indicated extended contact with Athabascan Indian chiefs of the Tanana region other than those of July 6 and 7, 1915:

> I spent the day [July 6] with 12 chiefs and headman of the Indians—from Salchaket to Ft. Gibbon...talking and advising them about Indian Hd. [?] & Reservations. They seem most opposed to reservations—Mr. Madara Episcopal minister is urging opposition to Reservations—Our whole days 'talk' is to be sent to Sec. of Interior Lane, in Washington & we will also write him about their wishes.

The July 7 entry reported: "Another long meeting with Indians today." An attached press clipping reported on the previous day's meeting: "The subject under discussion was the establishment of reservations for the Indians and how they could best protect themselves from the usual encroachment of the whites. The chiefs were a unit against reservations."

Stephen Langdon, by email on December 31, 2013, commented that the Tanana chiefs resisted because the reservation Wickersham suggested did not answer their aspirations. The chiefs wanted government protection from prospectors and trappers, but not government oversight.

62. Andrew Hope III, *Raven's Bones Journal* (1982): "An Interview with Judson Brown."

63. While Wickersham was a sincere supporter of Alaska Native causes, self-interest was also involved in his encouragement of Southeast Alaska Natives to seek recompense for lost lands. In 1929, Dan Sutherland chose not to run again for the position of delegate to Congress, and Wickersham was seeking Native votes in his campaign for the office he had held previous to Sutherland. He and Paul also discussed an arrangement by which they would collaborate on the suit and split a 15 percent commission. See Haycox, "Then Fight for It."

64. Mitchell, *Sold American*, 265.

65. Haycox, *Alaska: An American Colony*, 252.

66. For information about the 1932 campaign preferences of Wickersham and Dimond, see "Wickersham State Historic Site: Master Interpretive Plan,"

prepared for the Alaska State Office of History and Archaeology by Mary Pat Wyatt and Penny Bauder (2008).

67. Price, *The Great Father in Alaska*, 99.
68. In explaining the rift that was to develop between his father, Andrew P. Hope, and William Paul, John Hope said that it began when his father registered as a Democrat. His remembrance, offered during a KTOO-FM interview with the author's late father, Vern Metcalfe, in 1987, also explains in part the support Alaska Natives received from Republicans like Wickersham and Sutherland:

> In the early 1920s almost all of the Natives in Southeast were Republicans, almost all of them. And it was very common for Natives to be Republican and William Paul was Republican. Somewhere about the mid-1930s, my dad broke away from that party and went over to the Democratic side.... Because my father was held in such high regard it wasn't too long that most of the Natives in the Southeast were Democrats. Very few were left in the Republican party.

69. Price, *The Great Father in Alaska*, 92.
70. Ibid., 103.
71. Jurisdictional Act of June 19, 1935, 49 Stat. 388, ch. 295, subsequently amended by the Act of June 5, 1942, 56 Stat. 323 and Act of June 4, 1945, 59 Stat. 231. See also Peter Metcalfe, "An Historical & Organizational Profile: The Central Council of the Tlingit & Haida Indian Tribes of Alaska," 6.
72. Price, *The Great Father in Alaska*, 100.
73. Between William Paul and Delegate Dimond, a successful effort was mounted to extend the IRA to Alaska in 1936. As Dimond remarked in a report to Congress, the Alaska Native Brotherhood "at their own expense sent their secretary, Mr. William L. Paul, an attorney at law and a member of the Tlingit Tribe, to Washington to appear before the committee in support of the bill and the proposed amendments." The legislation passed, and within a few years Southeast Alaska Native communities were taking advantage of the revolving loan fund provided by the IRA (Price, *The Great Father in Alaska*, 105).

    Of the $10 million appropriated to the IRA fund, $4 million in loans were advanced to fund the purchase of canneries and boats in the Southeast Alaska villages of Kake, Angoon, Hydaburg, and Klawock. Decades later, one government report questioned why "forty percent of the funds appropriated by Congress for the financing of Indians is confined to four communities with a total estimated resident population of 1,445 persons when there are approximately 500,000 Indians in the United States" (ibid., 133).
74. Mitchell, *Sold American*, 308.
75. Ibid., 295.

76. Robert Price, a now-retired attorney who served as a federal solicitor during the early years of ANCSA and later as corporate attorney for a regional Native corporation, points out that, in adapting the IRA for Alaska, "Paul and Dimond took language from the credit union legislation and added 'common bond of residency,' which allowed Native villages to organize as tribes and receive loans from the revolving loan fund established by the IRA." See also Peter Metcalfe, *Gumboot Determination*, 224.

77. Haycox, "The 1935 Tlingit Haida Jurisdictional Act and the Alaska Native Claims Settlement Act of 1971: Promise and Denouement" (hereinafter "Promise and Denouement"), 3. The paper is attached to a letter addressed to Joaqlin Estus, September 3, 1986, found in the Andy Hope collection.

78. Mitchell, *Sold American*, 283. It should be noted here that in personal communications, Don Mitchell hotly disputed the somewhat neutral tone I have used regarding William Paul's disbarment. Mitchell finds Paul guilty, no equivocation about it. The author admits that Mitchell's research on the matter presents compelling evidence, but since there was no hearing on the disbarment, questions remain—most important, why Paul chose not to dispute the charge or, at the very least, attempt to salvage his license. Were he a white lawyer, it seems likely that, under the circumstances, the result may have been censure rather than disbarment. Through the efforts of his sons, Paul's license was reinstated in 1959.

79. A circular to ANB/ANS camps, dated February 28, 1950, by "(Mrs.) Margaret V. Thomas" of Klukwan, provides insight into why William Paul retained the support of so many ANB members and says something about the man himself:

> As many times he was defeated, he never give up. As for the Klukwan Camp, we have always voted a hundred percent for him.... Every time Paul writes circular letters, harsh and good ones, Klukwan receives one too and our people mumbles among themselves if it was a harsh letter and say "What did Klukwan do to Paul now? He should leave us alone." We get hurt just like anybody else, but in the meantime the elderly members always step in and talk to the younger group that if it wasn't for Paul, Sr., this organization would not be where it is now. He has fought a good fight for our people. We might as well admit it. (Paul family records)

80. Mitchell, *Sold American*, 354.

Chapter Three

81. The delegates elected to the Central Council included George Davis representing Angoon; Arthur Johnson, Craig; Annie Weaver, Douglas; John Mark, Haines; Gideon Duncan, Hydaburg; Jake Cropley, Juneau; Elizabeth

Baines, Ketchikan; Frank Peratrovich, Klawock; Robert Perkins, Klukwan; Frank Booth, Petersburg; Henry Denny Jr., Saxman; Frank Price, Sitka; Louis Paul, Wrangell; and Jack Ellis, Yakutat. David Morgan of Hoonah was elected chairman. Citations found in Andrew Hope III, *Raven's Bones Journal.*

82. Haycox, "Promise and Denouement," 14–23, and "Minutes of the April 9, 1941, meeting of the Tlingit-Haida Claims Committee," Paul family records.

83. While the original documents reprinted by Andy Hope in *Raven's Bones Journal* record the meeting date as November 16, 1935, Judson Brown, in a corresponding interview by Mr. Hope in the same journal, recalled the date as 1936.

84. The ANB's Resolution No. 37, passed at its 1939 convention, appointed the Grand Camp executive committee as the Tlingit and Haida Claims Committee for purposes of prosecuting the lawsuit permitted by the 1935 Jurisdictional Act. That Resolution No. 37 was seen by Department of Interior personnel as a provocation is revealed in the letter of June 13, 1940, by Deputy Interior Secretary Oscar L. Chapman to Claude M. Hirst, Juneau superintendent of the Office of Indian Affairs. The following paragraph from Chapman's letter provides a taste of the patronizing attitude that offended Alaska Natives so deeply that they would make just about any sacrifice to avoid such oversight:

> After the Tlingit and Haida Claims Committee has selected the desired attorneys and a proper contract has been executed, the function of the Committee will have been fully performed and neither it nor its members will have any further duties to perform or official connection with the prosecution of the claims of the tribes. The existence of the Tlingit and Haida Claims Committee will have terminated and its members may return to their homes. This explanation is being given so that it may clearly be understood that the authority and existence of this committee will not extend or continue beyond the employment of attorneys for and on behalf of the tribes in this initial instance. (Paul family records)

In spite of the Department of the Interior's directive, the Tlingit and Haida Claims Committee extended and continued, meeting and reorganizing at Wrangell in April 1941. In time, it became the Central Council of Tlingit and Haida Indian Tribes of Alaska, a federally recognized tribe that, in the late 1970s, began assuming most functions previously administered by the successor organization of Mr. Hirst's OIA—the Southeast Agency of the Bureau of Indian Affairs.

85. Haycox, "Promise and Denouement," 16.

86. Felix S. Cohen worked in the Solicitor's Office of the Department of the Interior from 1933 to 1947. He was a principal drafter of the Indian Reorganization Act and authored the seminal *Handbook of Federal Indian Law* (1941).

87. One of many examples documenting efforts by officials of the Department of the Interior to obstruct the lawsuit was reported by attorney James E. Curry in a circular sent to the ANB Grand Camp and local camps. Curry complained that the commissioner of Indian affairs, Dillon S. Meyer, refused to approve Curry's assignment of the case *Tlingit and Haida Indians of Alaska v. United States* to Weissbrodt, Hoag, Lindquist, et al., the firm that was to eventually bring the case before the U.S. Court of Claims. "Myers has nothing against any of these men [i.e., the lawyers]," Curry reported, "but is refusing approval merely to prevent you from prosecuting your claim." Curry had other axes to grind, especially that of his enmity towards William Paul Sr., but taken in the context of comments from other correspondents, including Interior department officials, it is obvious that interior officials had little tolerance for an Indian organization such as the ANB that refused to be controlled. (For quote see Curry circular, October 29, 1952; see also Curry circular of August 16, 1952, and William Paul Sr.'s November 3, 1952, speech to the ANB Grand Camp in reply to Curry, Paul family records.)

   On the other hand, Curry was more responsible for his fate than he let on. According to Haycox,

   > Curry had solicited Indian claims cases that he did not intend to work on himself. Rather, he had brokered them to other attorneys for a portion of their fees. In addition, he represented himself as holding [tribal] contracts before he actually had them, and he had colluded with his client's opponents without telling his clients. In 1952, the commissioner of Indian Affairs and the U.S. senator from New Mexico convened congressional hearings intended to expose Curry's allegedly unethical practices. When the hearings upheld many of the charges, the Indian office cancelled all of Curry's contracts. He was out of business. (Haycox, *Let Right Be Done*)

88. In the cultures of the Pacific Northwest, ownership was embodied in clans and clan houses. In this context, clan-owned property included land and buildings; hunting, harvesting, and fishing rights; ceremonial regalia and objects; and intellectual property such as clan histories and songs, all of which were recognized and validated at *koo.èex*. For an explanation of *at.óow* ("an owned or purchased thing or object") and the moiety-clan social structure, see Dauenhauers, *Haa Kusteeyí, Our Culture*, 3–23.

89. U.S. Constitution, Fifth Amendment: due process; Fourteenth Amendment: equal protection.

90. In a letter from William Paul Sr. to John Hope dated November 30, 1952, Paul makes his case for pursuing claims as clans, not as the collective Tlingit-Haida Indians of Alaska. His legal reasoning, he explains to Hope, is centered on the Fifth Amendment of the U.S. Constitution that prohibits the government from depriving a citizen of property without the due process of law. Most of the letter involves his recitation of actions taken by Curry, and Curry's supporters (Andrew Hope, Roy and Frank Peratrovich, and Frank Johnson), that led to the *Tlingit and Haida* lawsuit. As Paul expressed his reasoning to John Hope, "Tlingit" and "Haida" were language groups only, not entities that could claim ownership like clans, which were composed of U.S. citizens who therefore had claims to the lands and rights taken by the government without compensation.

    Paul was targeting the millions of dollars held in escrow as a result of the Tongass Timber Act of 1947. The lawyer fees would been substantial had he won, with the plaintiffs sharing the bulk of the money recovered from escrow. But who were the actual plaintiffs? J. C. Peacock, the attorney William Paul Sr. selected to represent *Tee-Hit-Ton*, in testimony before a congressional committee introduced himself as representing "six Alaska Indian clans and the individual heads or active leaders of at least ten other such clans." In extemporaneous remarks that followed his prepared statement, Peacock was grilled by Rep. Kenneth Regan (D-TX) and a Mr. Pillion (perhaps a staffer). "The five clans I represent have a membership roll of about 307-odd members." Questioned further about membership rolls, Peacock clearly had no idea as to numbers of people associated with clans and only a vague idea as to the number of clans. The follow-up questions and answers revealed the committee members' concerns about foisting such complexities upon the courts (testimony, Committee on Interior and Insular Affairs, 1/13/1954).

    In the modern era, clans have proved to be the appropriate recipients of *at.óow* (clan-owned property) such as the ceremonial objects that have been returned through the process authorized by the Native American Graves Protection and Repatriation Act of 1990 (NAGPRA). But cash is not sacred, and clans as they existed in the mid-1950s did not have the type of structure that would have permitted a distribution of cash satisfactory to all the possible claimants. At the time, there were about eight thousand self-identified Alaska Natives living in Southeast Alaska—how many considered themselves clan members cannot be known, but it is a safe assumption that, given a large cash settlement, there would have been many more claimants than the 307 members of various clans Peacock said he represented.

91. For legal citation of *Tee-Hit-Ton*, see "Cases Cited."
92. Haycox, "Then Fight For It."

93. For legal citation of *Tlingit and Haida Indians v. United States*, see Cases Cited.
94. Haycox, "Promise and Denouement," 69.
95. Ibid., 82.
96. Haycox, *Alaska: An American Colony*, 254.
97. Andrew P. Hope was referring to a decision by the U.S. Court of Claims, not the U.S. Supreme Court. Dauenhauers, *Haa Kusteeyí, Our Culture*, 266.
98. Haycox, "Promise and Denouement," 83.
99. Personal communication with the author, 1999. Quoted in Peter Metcalfe, *Earning a Place in History*, 22.
100. The settlement of Alaska Native claims came at the cost of closely held values for which money alone cannot compensate. But rough calculations can be made that compare the $7.5 million Tlingit-Haida award to the money and equity received by the Native people of Southeast Alaska through their participation in ANCSA. A crude analysis suggests that the twelve urban/village corporations plus Sealaska received in the neighborhood of $5 billion in equity (in early 1980s timber values) and distributed to shareholders, over time, more than $1 billion in cash (no adjustments for inflation). These summations do not include salaries, investments, and purchases by ANCSA corporations that contributed to the overall economy of Southeast Alaska.

    See Peter Metcalfe, *Earning a Place in History*, specifically the endnotes: "Original Shareholders," 89; "The Alaska Native Fund," 92; "Land Selection," 93; and "Timber Appraisal," 96. See also *Sealaska Annual Report 2011*, "Consolidated Financial Data," 30; and "Distributions," 34.
101. "Sealaska has received, or expects to receive, conveyance of approximately 362,000 acres of land in the Tongass National Forest in Southeast Alaska.... It is anticipated that the Village and Urban corporations in Sealaska's region will receive conveyance of 286,400 acres of land" (*Sealaska Annual Report 2012*, 49).

Chapter Four

102. *Verstovian* (Sheldon Jackson School newspaper), vol. 6, no. 2 (1919).
103. An anecdote recounted to the author by former Admiralty Island Monument manager K. J. Metcalf has the ring of truth: in the late 1970s, an elderly Tlingit man from Angoon was traveling to Washington, D.C., to testify before Congress during the Alaska Lands debate. In Seattle, the group went to a hotel to secure overnight accommodations. The desk clerk asked the elder if he had a reservation. "Reservation?" the old man replied indignantly. "I'm not a reservation Indian! I'm a free Indian!" (Personal communication, 2007).
104. Minutes of the April 9, 1941, meeting of the Tlingit-Haida Claims Committee (Paul family records).

105. Kan, *Memory Eternal*, 214; and personal communications with Stephen Langdon. According to Langdon, the missionaries' intent was to convince Alaska Natives they were separate from "Indians" of the continental U.S. to hasten acculturation. The following is from Langdon's email of September 10, 2012:

> The terminology "Alaska Native" and the geographic separation from the continental United States have both been used as reasons to ignore U.S. Indian Law and treaty precedent in order to block indigenous claims in Alaska, a situation similar to that faced by indigenous Hawaiians. Such distinctions are part of the reason there is such a problematic and confused landscape with regard to tribes and sovereignty in Alaska.

David Arnold, after citing the praise of several non-Natives for the industriousness of Southeast Alaska Natives, writes:

> While such glowing depictions undoubtedly reflected the extent to which Indians were successfully navigating the market economy [in the late nineteenth century], talk of self-supporting Indians also served as a ready argument against extending the federal reservation system to Alaska, which, many non-Indians feared, would quarantine the region's natural resources and stymie industrial enterprise. (Arnold, *The Fishermen's Frontier*, 71)

106. Mitchell, *Sold American*, 287.

107. See "Gravina Island Bridge," http://en.wikipedia.org/wiki/Gravina_Island_Bridge.

108. Minutes of the Tlingit-Haida Claims Committee, April 9, 1941 (Paul family records).

109. Letter dated November 6, 1946 (Paul family records).

110. Mitchell, *Sold American*, 287–351.

111. Paul, *Then Fight for It*, 107.

112. Richard Hanna, a former chief justice of the New Mexico Supreme Court, was considered an Indian law expert (Price, *The Great Father*, 113).

113. Haycox, "Promise and Denouement," 26.

114. Hanna hearings, vol. III, 461–63.

115. Haycox, "Promise and Denouement," 26.

116. Ibid.

117. Ibid., 36–37.

118. Price, *The Great Father in Alaska*, 128.

119. Thomas, "Alaska Statehood: A Southeast Alaska Native Perspective."

120. Price, 131–132.

121. *Ketchikan Daily News*, 1950 clipping in the Soboleff collection, Sealaska Heritage Institute.

122. Ibid.
123. Price, *The Great Father in Alaska*, 133.
124. Ibid.

Chapter Five

125. Rogers, *Alaska Native Population Trends and Vital Statistics: 1950–1985.* The 2010 census reported that the number of Alaskans who identify as Native American grew by 16 percent in the first decade of the twenty-first century. In 2010, Alaska Natives and other Native Americans living in Alaska numbered 138,312, or 24.2 percent of the total population. See www.census.gov/prod/cen2010/briefs/c2010br-10.pdf.
126. Mitchell, *Sold American*, 388.
127. Ibid., 378.
128. The "trust relationship" with Native Americans developed after the U.S. Supreme Court recognized tribes as "domestic dependent nations" subject to federal oversight and protection. Through this trust relationship, the U.S. government acts as a fiduciary. In the territory of Alaska, in absence of a formal federal recognition of Alaska tribes, the federal government recognized that a trust relationship existed. Hence, the U.S. government took responsibility for education, health care, and, where applicable, land management for Alaska Natives. The Indian Self-Determination Act of 1975 brought fundamental changes to the trust relationship by allowing the transfer of administrative responsibility for Native American programs to tribes and tribal entities.
129. In 1950, 46 percent of all Alaska Native deaths were caused by infectious disease, compared to only 3 percent for the non-Native population. See Peter Metcalfe, *Gumboot Determination*, 41; Fortuine, *Must We All Die?*, 132–36; also see http://www.hss.state.ak.us/dph/targets/PDFs/history2000.pdf.
130. Dauenhauers, *Haa Kusteeyí, Our Culture*, 538. Elizabeth was married to Roy, brother of Frank Peratrovich. Elizabeth Peratrovich's rebuttals of challenges by a senator read like well-scripted responses, and indeed they were, according to research by Ishmael Hope:

> As Roy described it, they planned out every question they thought might be asked, and they rehearsed their answers. Elizabeth's testimony was masterful in its rhetoric, in its appeals to the greatest American ideals, and in its surgically precise destruction of the faulty, foolish logic of racial discrimination. As my grandfather John used to say, "We used the white man's tools to help our people." This is one of the finest examples we have on record. There were other examples, too. It took a whole community to do this important work. (Ishmael Hope, http://alaskanativestoryteller.com/blog/page/5/)

131. Interview by Stephen Langdon with Edward Thomas, July 21, 2009.

132. Haycox, *Alaska: An American Colony*, 269.

133. Between the world wars, pioneering American military aviators like General Billy Mitchell recognized the geographical significance of Alaska, the only American possession centrally located along air routes to the continental United States from Asia, Europe, and much of the Pacific Rim. In 1949, the Soviet Union developed the atomic bomb, ending the United States' four-year nuclear hegemony. Missile delivery systems had yet to be developed, and, for the next decade, intercontinental bombers represented the means by which the two superpowers threatened each other with nuclear Armageddon. By virtue of geography, Alaska became the front line in the nuclear standoff.

134. House Concurrent Resolution 108 (1953). As indicated by a note typed on a copy of H.C.R. 108, William Paul Sr. favored including Southeast Alaska in the termination language of the resolution, apparently to clarify the basis of *Tee-Hit-Ton*, which held that Alaska Natives were American citizens (not tribal members) whose property had been taken from them by the U.S. government without compensation. Paul had long opposed the concept of tribes in Alaska. He equated tribalism with wardship and a rebuke to his concept of the property rights he was trying to establish in *Tee-Hit-Ton*. (Paul family records)

135. See http://www.aaanativearts.com/terminated_tribes.htm.

136. Wilkinson, *Blood Struggle*, 57.

Chapter Six

137. Mitchell, *Sold American*, 365.

138. Haycox, "Then Fight for It."

139. The Tongass Timber Act of 1947 began its legislative life as House Joint Resolution 205.

140. Mitchell, *Sold American*, 385.

141. Ibid., 409.

142. Ibid., 395.

143. Ibid., 394.

144. Ibid., 393.

145. Ibid., 398.

146. Ibid., 413.

147. Harold Ickes to Interior Secretary Oscar Chapman, July 4, 1950; Harold Ickes to Sen. Joseph Mahoney, July 4, 1950 (Paul family records). Whether or not Senator Mahoney ever had a conversation with William Paul Sr., he accurately reflected Paul's insistence that Alaska Natives were U.S. citizens rather than members of a tribe. By this time (1950), Paul was fully invested in his theory that Alaska Natives were citizens who had had their

land and rights taken from them by the U.S. government without compensation. This view put Paul squarely in opposition to James Curry, many ANB members, and non-Native allies like Ickes. Paul's belief differed from the common interpretation that Indians were not included in the 14th Amendment grant of citizenship because they were not subject to U.S. jurisdiction at the time that amendment became law.

148. The remarks of James Curry and Gov. Ernest Gruening are found in the minutes of the thirty-eighth annual ANB/ANS Grand Camp convention at Craig, Alaska, November 13–18, 1950. The minutes are near-verbatim transcriptions of the remarks made, questions asked, and the responses. Walter Soboleff collection, Sealaska Heritage Institute, Juneau, Alaska.

See also Governor Gruening's testimony to Congress on February 11, 1952, which, in addition to his perception of the social and economic standing of Alaska Natives, includes his speech to the 1950 ANB Grand Camp convention (Congressional Record).

149. ANB Grand Camp convention records, Walter Soboleff collection, Sealaska Heritage Institute.

150. Soboleff collection, Sealaska Heritage Institute.

151. Ibid.

Chapter Seven

152. Mitchell, *Sold American*, 399.

153. William Paul Sr., initially not opposed to Curry, soon became an antagonist over philosophical differences and disagreements of legal theory and tactics. Original correspondence found in the Paul family records attests to the intense animosity. By the early 1950s, each was accusing the other of lying, unethical behavior, and ignorance of basic legal concepts. The elder Paul had a web of correspondents who provided him with copies of private letters from Curry to individual ANB members.

154. Minutes of the thirty-ninth annual ANB/ANS Grand Camp convention at Ketchikan, Alaska, November 1951, Andrew Hope III collection.

155. Unpublished U.S. Senate Hearings, CIS Index to 18-84 Congress, 1833–1964, Vol. 6, 617.

156. Ibid., 619.

157. James Curry, circular to ANB annual convention, October 29, 1952 (Paul family records).

158. William Paul Sr., "To the Alaska Native Brotherhood & Sisterhood," November 3, 1952 (Paul family records).

159. Paul, *Then Fight for It*, 127.

160. Ibid.

161. Mitchell, *Sold American*, 424.

162. Ibid., 434.

163. Circular to all ANB and ANS members from Grand Secretary Peter Nielsen, April 4, 1953 (Paul family records).
164. "Urging Alaska Natives Be Heard on H.R. 1921, Possessory Claims Bill," 1953 NCAI convention (Paul family records).
165. The couple, Roy (1908–1989) and Elizabeth (1911–1958) Peratrovich, made it their lifetime mission to win, then protect and extend, civil rights for all Alaska Natives. An impressive archive of correspondence, news clippings, and other material that documents their relentless efforts on behalf of all Alaska Natives can be found under the family name at the University of Alaska Anchorage library.

    In 1988, the Alaska Legislature established February 16, the anniversary of the signing of Alaska's Anti-Discrimination Act of 1945, as Elizabeth Peratrovich Day.

    Those who know the complete story understand that many more people than Elizabeth Peratrovich alone deserve recognition. But Mrs. Peratrovich—elegant and articulate—serves, as have other historical figures, as an admirable icon for one of those major steps forward that have advanced human rights.
166. One of many condescending and hectoring letters written by William Paul Sr. to John Hope is that of September 9, 1954: "I have wondered if you sincerely believe that you can perform the duties of your office better than I. Could you write such a letter as this?" So begins a note attached to a letter Paul wrote on the same day to Secretary of the Interior Douglas McKay. A full letter to Hope, also written on the same day, concludes as follows: "My resentment at your occupation of your office [Grand Camp secretary] is not due to anything that concerns me personally, but because you have a wonderful opportunity for serving your people and you are not doing it. I have always been willing to help, or at least, I would be most happy if you applied yourself to this important business" (Paul family records).
167. Correspondence to Frank Booth (Grand Camp executive committee member), February 6, 1957 (Paul family records).
168. Elizabeth Peratrovich (Juneau, AK) to Helen L. Peterson (Denver, CO), November 30, 1953 correspondence (Paul family records).
169. The purpose of the version of H.R. 1921 the ANB debated was to settle the claims of Southeast Alaska Natives through compensation for extinguished claims, and the issuance of title to Natives for property they occupied (their homesites) or used (such as fish camps and smoke houses). As Paul summarized in the circular, the ANB wanted amendments that would (1) have "Community of Natives" inserted alongside of "Indian Tribes" to clarify the confusion in a region where there were no federally recognized tribes; (2) extend from two to five years the statute of limitations to make claims; (3) assure that attorney fees would not create liabilities for Native

claimants; (4) retain the power of the secretary of the interior to establish reservations; (5) add the phrase "fair and honorable dealings" in the settlement of claims; and (6) eliminate the double standard required of Indian claimants. Paul expressed confidence that most of these amendments would prevail, but he thought point four was unattainable: "the bill will fail if the Secretary's power is not abolished." He believed point five acceptable but unnecessary, since the bill's purpose was to assure a fair deal; and point six meaningless because "even after the bill is amended, Indians will still be required to carry the burden of proof" to claim compensation for lands taken by trespass. Bill Paul Jr. to ANB Grand Camp executive committee, January 5, 1954 (Paul family records).

170. Mitchell, *Sold American*, 402.
171. Paul to Mr. Peacock, January 19, 1954 (Paul family records).
172. Helen Peterson (1915–2000) was an Oglala Dakota (Sioux) born on the Pine Ridge reservation. From 1953 to 1961 she served as the executive director of the National Congress of American Indians in Washington, D.C. Peterson helped rally opposition to the termination legislation introduced in Congress aimed at ending Native American sovereignty. She organized tribal leaders to fight the policy and helped conduct voting drives to elect Democrats sympathetic to the tribes' cause. Widely recognized for her efforts, in 1973 she was awarded an honorary doctorate of humane letters from the University of Colorado.
173. Peterson to Elizabeth Peratrovich and John Hope on January 23, 1954. Peterson apparently had a personal relationship with Elizabeth Peratrovich (she offered to put up Elizabeth's husband, Roy, at her home if he had to travel to D.C., and added a postscript, "Mother says hello!") (Paul family records).
174. Patrick Paul to John Hope, February 6, 1954, correspondence (Paul family records).
175. Mitchell, *Sold American*, 404.
176. Ibid., 406.
177. Ibid., 404.
178. Ibid., 419–20.
179. For the day sixty-four floor debate relevant to the disclaimer clause (Section 4), see the Alaska Constitutional Convention Minutes, at www.law.alaska.gov/doclibrary/conconv/64.html.
180. Alaska Statehood Act, Section 4:

As a compact with the United States said State and its people do agree and declare that they forever disclaim all right and title to any lands or other property not granted or confirmed to the State or its political subdivisions by or under the authority of this Act, the right or title to which is held by the United States or

is subject to disposition by the United States, and to any lands
or other property, (including fishing rights), the right or title to
which may be held by any Indians, Eskimos, or Aleuts (hereinafter called natives) or is held by the United States in trust
for said natives; that all such lands or other property, belonging to the United States or which may belong to said natives,
shall be and remain under the absolute jurisdiction and control
of the United States until disposed of under its authority, except to such extent as the Congress has prescribed or may hereafter prescribe, and except when held by individual natives in
fee without restrictions on alienation: Provided, That nothing
contained in this act shall recognize, deny, enlarge, impair, or
otherwise affect any claim against the United States, and any
such claim shall be governed by the laws of the United States
applicable thereto; and nothing in this Act is intended or shall
be construed as a finding, interpretation, or construction by the
Congress that any law applicable thereto authorizes, establish-
es, recognizes, or confirms the validity or invalidity of any such
claim, and the determination of the applicability or effect of any
law to any such claim shall be unaffected by anything in this
Act: And provided further, That no taxes shall be imposed by
said State upon any lands or other property now owned or hereafter acquired by the United States or which, as hereinabove set
forth, may belong to said natives, except to such extent as the
Congress has prescribed or may hereafter prescribe, and except
when held by individual natives in fee without restrictions on
alienation. (www.lbblawyers.com/statc4.htm)

181. Haycox, "Alaska Should Celebrate 'Bartlett Day.'"
182. While a student at Mt. Edgecumbe in Sitka, Charlie "Etok" Edwardsen took a
pilgrimage to Wrangell to meet the famous William Paul, who instructed the
young Inupiat in the history of Alaska Native claims (Gallagher, *Etok,* 120).
183. Ibid., 120–21.
184. Ibid., 123.
185. Mitchell, *Take My Land, Take My Life,* 129–31.
186. Ibid., 148.

Chapter Eight

187. A common retrospective point of view has underestimated the challenges
that confronted ANB leaders from the organization's inception through
the Alaska statehood movement era. In his memoir, *Fifty Miles from Tomorrow,* Willie Hensley, an Alaska Native leader from Kotzebue and now
Anchorage who participated in the ANCSA lobbying effort by the Alaska

Federation of Natives, an organization he later led, gives no credit to the fifty-year-long struggle of Southeast Alaska Natives on behalf of Alaska aboriginal claims. The only reference is found on page 127, where Hensley writes about his impressions immediately after he was elected to the Alaska legislature in 1964:

> I wasn't the first Native Alaskan in the legislature, but there had not been many others, and I was certainly one of the first of my generation. Earlier Native legislators had become Americanized, accepting of the status quo, and unwilling to fight for their people's land. The new generation was different. Backed by passionate supporters, we were determined to use our youthful energy to make major changes.

Anyone well informed in Alaska's political history would know that Mr. Hensley's statement dismisses the critical contributions of William Paul Sr., Andrew P. Hope, Frank Peratrovich, and Frank G. Johnson, Tlingits who had served in the legislature prior to Hensley and who were all stalwart leaders of the Alaska Native Brotherhood. These men, among others, fought tenacious battles to win civil rights for Alaska Natives and to preserve the aboriginal claims by which Hensley later made his name.

To Hensley's credit, his 1966 essay, "What Rights to Land Have the Alaska Native: The Primary Question," set forth historical precedents for Alaska Native claims. Produced for a graduate class in constitutional law taught by Alaska Supreme Court Justice Jay Rabinowitz several months prior to the formation of the Alaska Federation of Natives, the essay is widely credited as a foundational document of the effort to settle Alaska Native claims following statehood.

188. See *Tlingit and Haida Indians of Alaska v. The United States* (http://openjurist.org/389/f2d/778).

189. Early in 1968, AFN president Emil Notti presided at the meeting at which the question of including Southeast Alaska in the statewide Native claims settlement effort was decided. In 1999, in a personal communication with the author, as quoted in *Earning a Place in History*, Notti recounted how the issue was resolved: "At the time, we had a twenty-five-person board. We had a hot argument; even our lawyers were jumping in, and finally, we had to clear the room and have an executive session. The argument against including [the Tlingit-Haida people] was that they already had a settlement, and that including them would weaken our position. The argument in favor was that they didn't get a fair settlement. We wanted to help them get a fair settlement, and with them, there would be strength in unity." The board was split, and Notti cast the tie-breaking vote. See Peter Metcalfe, *Earning a Place in History*, "Land Selection," 93.

190. Remarks by Emil Notti during a presentation recognizing the one-hundredth anniversary of the Alaska Legislature on March 3, 2013, in the Juneau Elks Club Hall, where the first legislature convened.

191. Presentation by John Borbridge and Emil Notti at the Alaska State Library in Juneau, December 3, 2009.

References

Arnold, David F. *The Fishermen's Frontier: People and Salmon in Southeast Alaska.* Seattle: University of Washington Press, 2008.

Bancroft, Hubert Howe. *The Works of Hubert Howe Bancroft: History of Alaska.* San Francisco: A. L. Bancroft & Publishers, 1886. Google Books edition, November 2007.

Bettridge, Dr. Joseph. *The Emergence of Tlingit Christianity.* Pasadena: Fuller Theological Seminary, 1979.

Case, David S., and David A. Voluck. *Alaska Natives and American Laws* (2nd ed.). Fairbanks: University of Alaska Press, 2002.

Catton, Theodore. *Inhabited Wilderness.* Albuquerque: University of New Mexico Press, 1997.

Cohen, Felix. *Handbook of Federal Indian Law.* Washington, D. C.: United States Government Printing Office, 1941.

Dauenhauer, Nora Marks, and Richard Dauenhauer. *Haa Kusteeyí, Our Culture: Tlingit Life Stories.* Juneau: Sealaska Heritage Foundation, 1994.

de Laguna, Frederica. *The Tlingit Indians.* Seattle: University of Washington Press, 1991.

Fortuine, Robert. *Must We All Die? Alaska's Enduring Struggle with Tuberculosis.* Fairbanks: University of Alaska Press, 2005.

Gallagher, Hugh Gregory. *Etok: A Story of Eskimo Power.* New York: G. P. Putnam's Sons, 2001.

Goldschmidt, Walter R., and Theodore H. Haas. *Haa Aaní (Our Land): Tlingit and Haida Land Rights and Use.* Juneau: Sealaska Heritage Foundation, 1998.

Gruening, Ernest. *The Battle for Alaska Statehood.* Fairbanks: University of Alaska Press, 1967.

Haycox, Stephen W. "1935 Tlingit Haida Jurisdictional Act and the Alaska Native Claims Settlement Act of 1971: Promise and Denouement." Essay/correspondence with Joaqlin Estus, 3 September 1986, found in the Andy Hope collection.

———. *Alaska: An American Colony.* Seattle: University of Washington Press, 2002.

———. "Alaska Should Celebrate 'Bartlett Day.'" *Anchorage Daily News*, April 29, 2010.

———. *Let Right Be Done: Aboriginal Title, the Calder Case, and the Future of Indigenous Rights.* Hamar Foster, Heather Raven, and Jeremy Webber, eds. Vancouver, B.C.: University of British Columbia Press, 2007.

———. "Then Fight for It: William Lewis Paul and Alaska Native Land Claims." Paper for the "Let Right Be Done" conference, University of Victoria, November 2003.

Hensley, William L. Iggiagruk. *Fifty Miles from Tomorrow.* New York: Farrar, Straus and Giroux, 2008.

———. "What Rights to Land Have the Alaska Natives? The Primary Question," May 1966. Available at www.alaskool.org/projects/ancsa/wlh/wlh66-all-bigtype.pdf.

Hinkley, Ted C. *The Canoe Rocks: Alaska's Tlingit and the Euramerican Frontier, 1800–1912.* Landham: University Press of America.

Hope, Andrew "Andy" III. "On the Organization of the Tlingit and Haida Central Council: An Interview with Judson Brown." *Raven's Bones Journal,* 1982.

Hope, Andrew "John." "History of the Alaska Native Brotherhood." Unpublished manuscript, 1998.

Hope, Ishmael. "They Won't Be Forgotten: The Leaders of the Alaska Native Brotherhood and Sisterhood." February 18, 2012. Available at http://alaskanativestoryteller.com/blog/page5.

Isto, Sarah Crawford. *The Fur Farms of Alaska: Two Centuries of History and a Forgotten Stampede.* Fairbanks: University of Alaska Press, 2012.

Kan, Sergei. *Memory Eternal: Tlingit Culture and Russian Orthodox Christianity through Two Centuries.* Fairbanks: University of Alaska Press, 1999.

———. *A Russian American Photographer in Tlingit Country: Vincent Soboleff in Alaska.* Norman: University of Oklahoma Press, 2013.

Langdon, Stephen. "Honoring Our Founders: Carrying Their Vision Forward." Keynote address, ANB/ANS Grand Camp convention, Sitka, October 2, 2012.

———. *The Native People of Alaska,* 3rd edition. Anchorage: Greatland Graphics, 1993.

Light, David P. *Brothers in Harmony: The Haines Alaska Native Brotherhood Founders.* Anchorage: David P. Light, 2002.

Mackovjak, James. *Alaska Salmon Traps.* James Mackovjak, 2013.

Metcalfe, Kim, ed. *In Sisterhood: The History of Camp 2 of the Alaska Native Sisterhood.* Juneau: Hazy Island Books, 2008.

Metcalfe, Peter. "An Historical & Organizational Profile: The Central Council of the Tlingit & Haida Indian Tribes of Alaska." Juneau: Central Council of the Tlingit & Haida Indian Tribes of Alaska, 1981.

———. *Earning a Place in History: Shee Atiká*, 2nd edition. Sitka: Sitka Native Claims Corporation, Shee Atiká, 2011.

———. *Gumboot Determination: The Story of the Southeast Alaska Regional Health Consortium.* Juneau: SEARHC, 2005.

Mitchell, Donald Craig. *Take My Land, Take My Life: The Story of Congress's Historic Settlement of Alaska Native Land Claims, 1960–1971.* Fairbanks: University of Alaska Press, 2001.

———. *Sold American: The Story of Alaska Natives and their Land, 1867–1959.* Fairbanks: University of Alaska Press, 2003.

Olson, Wallace M. *Through Spanish Eyes: The Spanish Voyages to Alaska, 1774–1792.* Auke Bay: Heritage Research, 2002.

Paul, Fred. *Then Fight for It: The Largest Peaceful Redistribution of Wealth in the History of Mankind.* Seattle: Fred Paul, 2003.

Price, Robert E. *The Great Father in Alaska: The Case of the Tlingit and Haida Salmon Fishery.* Juneau: First Street Press, 1990.

Rogers, George W. *Alaska Native Population Trends and Vital Statistics: 1950–1985.* Fairbanks: Institute of Social, Economic, and Government Research, November 1971.

Shales, Joyce Walton. "Rudolph Walton: One Man's Journey Through Stormy Seas." Doctoral thesis, University of British Columbia, 1998.

Thomas, Edward K. "Alaska Statehood: A Southeast Alaska Native Perspective." Sealaska Heritage Institute, April 2010.

"Verstovian," Sheldon Jackson School Newspaper, 1914–1973.

Wilkinson, Charles. *Blood Struggle: The Rise of Modern Indian Nations.* New York: W. W. Norton & Co., 2005.

Worl, Rosita. "The Birth of the Civil Rights Movement." *Alaska Native News*, November 1983.

Wyatt, Mary Pat and Penny Bauder. *The Wickersham State Historic Site: Master Interpretive Plan.* Anchorage: Alaska State Office of History and Archaeology, 2008.

Cases Cited

Tee-Hit-Ton Indians v. United States, 120 F. Supp. 202, 128 Ct. Cl. 82 (legal citation for the Court of Claims decision April 6, 1954); 348 U.S. 272, 75 S.Ct. 313, 99 L.Ed. 314, reh. denied, 348 U.S. 965, 75 S.Ct. 521, 99 L.Ed. 753 (legal citation for the decision of the U.S. Supreme Court issued February 7, 1955). For web link see http://supreme.justia.com/us/348/272/case.html.

Tlingit and Haida Indians of Alaska v. United States, 177 F. Supp. 452, 147 Ct. Cl. 315 (legal citation for the decision of the Court of Claims issued Oct. 7, 1959, which held that the Tlingit and Haida people "as a tribe, had established aboriginal Indian title … by their exclusive use and occupancy of that territory from time immemorial"; and 389 F. 2d 778 (legal citation for the Court of Claims decision on Jan. 19, 1968, setting the amount of the recovery award for lands taken). For web link see http://openjurist.org/389/f2d/778.

Organized Village of Kake v. Egan, 369 U.S. 60, 82 S.Ct. 562, 7 L.Ed.2d 573 (1962). For web link see http://openjurist.org/369/us/60/organized-village-of-kake-v-a-egan.

About the Author
and Researchers

Peter Metcalfe, writer/publisher, communications specialist, and lifelong resident of Juneau, has worked for every major Native organization in Southeast Alaska, including most of the region's Alaska Native Claims Settlement Act corporations, producing books, newsletters, annual reports, and video documentaries.

Kathy Kolkhorst Ruddy, attorney and researcher, received her JD from the University of Connecticut Law School in 1977. She began her career in law as a clerk for Justice Robert Boochever of the Alaska Supreme Court. Later, she began working for the State of Alaska Department of Law as an assistant attorney general. In 1986, she entered private practice with Ruddy Bradley and Kolkhorst, a Juneau law firm. Her interest in Alaska Native culture found expression during her service as a volunteer producer for *Southeast Native Radio*, a weekly show broadcast on KTOO-FM that ran from 1985 to 2001.

Stephen Langdon, project advisor, retired on June 30, 2014, as professor and chair of the Department of Anthropology at the University of Alaska Anchorage. For more than thirty years, Dr. Langdon has conducted research in ecological anthropology, economic anthropology, and ethnohistory of Northwest Coast maritime societies.

Index

Note: Italicized page numbers indicate illustrations and their captions.

AAIA (Association on American Indian
  Affairs), xix
"abandonment" of land, 67, 69
aboriginal claims, 7–8, 62, 68
  See also Alaska Native claims; Alaska
    Native Claims Settlement Act, 1971
    (ANCSA)
aboriginal rights concept, xix, xx, 21, 55, 60
aboriginal title
  ANB and, xxiii
  assertion of, to land north of Brooks
    Range, 85
  and citizenship for Alaska Natives, 21
  extinguishment bills, 2, 66–69, 74
  failure of U.S. government to recognize,
    7
  issue of treaties and, 88
  legal basis for, in Alaska, 8–10, 38
  significance discounted by politicians,
    39–40
  Tee-Hit-Ton Indians v. United States as
    confirmation of, 83
  treaties and, 26
  as unresolved issue in Alaska, 65, 88
  U.S. Forest Service and, 66
  Western legal theory of, 1–2
AFN (Alaska Federation of Nations), *xxi*,
  xxii–xxiii, 87–88, 93n7
Ahtna, Inc , *xxii*
Alaska
  congressional delegation, 91n3
  geostrategic significance of, 61,
    114n133
  oil lease sales and land selections by
    State of, 84–85
  Russian era in, 13–14, 98–99n34,
    100n38
  Spanish expeditions to, 100n38
Alaska Constitutional Convention (1955–
  1956), 57, 84

Alaska Federation of Nations (AFN), *xxi*,
  xxii–xxiii, 87–88, 93n7
Alaska National Interest Lands Conservation, 1980 (ANILCA), xx, 7, 91n3
Alaska Native Brotherhood (ANB)
  aboriginal title in Alaska and, xxiii
  anti-Paul faction, 31
  assimilation and, 14
  Camp #1, 102n50
  consultations on legislation to reform
    U.S. Indian policy, 28
  cultural accommodation by founders
    of, 15–16
  focus of, 4, 6, 8, 13, 21, 48
  formation of Tlingit-Haida Central
    Council, 35–36
  founders of, 13, 15–16, 98n31
  John Hope on history of, 23, 99n36
  independence from white religious
    leaders, 19
  indispensability of, 11, 87–89
  initial organizing effort by, 35
  William Paul, Sr. and, 20–21, 25, 82,
    107n79
  perspective on reservations, 45–47,
    51–52, 54, 70
  representation in Washington, 25,
    81–82
  Peter Simpson as "father" of, 14–15
  Sitka #1 camp, 102n50
  stance on rejection of Native traditions
    and language, 19
  See also ANB/ANS Grand Camp
    Conventions
Alaska Native claims
  AFN and, xxii–xxiii
  allotment claims as of 1970, 4
  Cold War and, *61*
  Congressional acts addressing property
    rights, 4

movement for, 6, 23
as obstacle to statehood, 75
omitted from Alaska statehood bills,
66, 69–70
settlement of, 10, 111n100
State of Alaska's disregard for, 84–85
U.S. government's disregard for, 21
See also Alaska Native Claims
Settlement Act, 1971 (ANCSA)
Alaska Native Claims Bill (H.R. 4388),
75, 78
Alaska Native Claims Settlement Act, 1971
(ANCSA)
ANB and, xxiii
circumstances contributing to passage
of, 88–89
debates of 1960s, 7
flaws in, 43
origins of, 103–105n57
political influence of Alaska Natives
following passage of, 92–93n7
precursors of, 50–51
regional, village, and urban
corporations, *xxii* (map), 92n6
Section 17(d)(2), xx
as social experiment, xxii
Alaska Natives
adapt/perish choice, 15
considered "uncivilized," 18–19
elected to serve in first state legislature,
56
interests of, in post-World War II
period, xix–xx
occupancy and use rights of, ignored by
Congress, 4
opposition to reclaiming rights to land,
48
population and representation at Alaska
Constitutional Convention, 57
preexisting rights issue, 26
relationship with U.S. government, 58
strategies employed to accommodate
pressures of white society, 16–17
as term, origins and use of, 46
Alaska Native Sisterhood (ANS), *xvi*, xix,
19, 91n2
See also ANB/ANS Grand Camp
Conventions
Alaska Native Townsite Act, 4–6
Alaska Salmon Commission, 3
Alaska Salmon Fisheries Act (ASFA), 3
Alaska Statehood Act (S. 49), *xxi*, 83–84,
92n6, 117–118n180

Alaska statehood bills, 57, 66, 69–73
Alaska statehood movement
aboriginal rights and, 55
Alaska Native claims as obstacle, 75
Alaska Natives and, 58
ANB as obstacle to, xix–xx
fish traps and, 60
in postwar period, 10, 57
support for, xx
Alaska State Legislature (1959), 56
Aleut Corporation, *xxii*
Allotment Act (1906), 4
allotment claims by Alaska Natives as of
1970, 4
American exceptionalism, 61–62
ANB. *See* Alaska Native Brotherhood
(ANB)
ANB/ANS couple, Jack and Emma Ellis, *12*
ANB/ANS Grand Camp Conventions
1914, Sitka, 19
1920, Wrangell, 20–21
1929, Haines, *xvi*, 8, 23–25
1930, Ketchikan, *24*
1930s, Sitka, *22*
1939, Sitka, 35
1944, Kake, 50
1946, Wrangell, *9*
1947, Hydaburg, 51
1950, Craig, 70, 72–73
1951, Ketchikan, 76
2012, 103n57
ANCSA. *See* Alaska Native Claims
Settlement Act, 1971 (ANCSA)
Anderson, Edward, *59*
ANILCA (Alaska National Interest Lands
Conservation, 1980), xx, 7, 91n3
Annette Island Reserve, *44*, 46–48, 52, 53,
71, 97n27
ANS (Alaska Native Sisterhood), *xvi*, xix,
19, 91n2
See also ANB/ANS Grand Camp
Conventions
Anti-Discrimination Act (1945), 54, 58–59,
96n25, 116n165
Arctic Slope Regional Corporation, *xxii*
Arnold, David, 3, 7, 95n22, 112n105
Arnold, W.C., 49
ASFA (Alaska Salmon Fisheries Act), 3
assimilation argument, 14–15, 52, 61–62,
100n36
Association on American Indian Affairs
(AAIA), xix

Bancroft, Hubert Howe, 103–105n57
Bartlett, E.L. "Bob"
  as advocate for Alaska Natives, 58
  Alaska statehood and, xx, 57
  and disclaimer clause to statehood bill,
    83–84
  H.R. 206 introduced by, 66
  H.R. 4388 introduced by, 75
  opposition to reservations in Southeast,
    52–54
  views on aboriginal claims, 68
Bartlett Land Bill (H.R. 4388), 75, 78
Bergt, Laura, 86
Bering Straits Native Corporation, xxii
Bettridge, Joseph, 98n30
Borbridge, John, Jr., 40–41, 86, 88
Bristol Bay Native Corporation, xxii
Brown, Judson, 20, 23–25
Bureau of Indian Affairs, 30
  See also Office of Indian Affairs (OIA)
Butler, Hugh, 70, 83

Calista Corporation, xxii, 20
Carlisle Indian School, Pennsylvania, 20
Carter, Jimmy, 91n3
Central Council of Tlingit and Haida
  Indian Tribes of Alaska (CCTHITA)
    delegates elected to, 107–108n81
    as full-fledged organization
      independent of ANB, 40–41
    as interim board of directors for
      Sealaska Corporation, 41–43
    judgment award in Tlingit and Haida,
      39–40, 88
    loan to AFN, 41, 88
    See also Tlingit-Haida Central Council
      (Tlingit-Haida Claims Committee)
Chapman, Oscar, 36
choke setters, Kuiu Island, 64
Chugach Natives, Inc., xxii
citizenship for Alaska Natives, as focus of
  ANB, 8, 13, 21
civil rights for Alaska Natives, 13
  See also Anti-Discrimination Act (1945)
clans, and clan-owned property, 110n90
Cobb, David, 37, 39, 77
Cochran, O.D., 59
Cohen, Felix S., 26, 29–30, 65, 109n86
Cold War, 61
Collier, John, 26, 28–30
commercial fishing industry
  Alaska Natives and, 3
  fish traps, 21, 25, 27–28, 49, 59–60

Cook Inlet Region, Inc., xxii
Cottages, The, 17–19
cultural accommodation, and self-
  determination, 15
Curry, James E., 74
  animosity between William Paul and,
    115n153
  on attempts by Department of the
    Interior to obstruct lawsuit, 109n87
  as general counsel for NCAI, 36
  opposition to H.R. 331, 70–71, 73
  opposition to H.R. 4388, 75–76
  opposition to H.R. 7002, 68
  testimony before Congress on
    statehood bill, 66
  Tlingit and Haida lawsuit, 65
  as unsung hero, 77

d-2 [Section 17(d)(2) of ANCSA], xx
Dalton, George, 21
Dauenhauer, Richard and Nora, 13–14
Davis, Mary, 17–18
Davis v. Sitka School Board, 18
Demmert, Charles Webster, 102n56
Department of Justice, 80
Department of the Interior
  attempts to obstruct Tlingit and Haida
    lawsuit, 109n87
  authorization for establishment of
    reservations by, 45–46, 55, 65
  H.R. 1921 amendments proposed by,
    80, 82
  reservations created by, 48, 51
Dimond, Anthony "Tony," 26–28, 30,
  106n73
Doyon, Ltd., xxii
Duncan, Father, 44

education, 18, 20, 98n34
Edwardsen, Charlie, Jr. "Etok," 85, 118n182
Egan, Bill, 39–40, 85
Eisenhower, Dwight, 55, 57, 60, 84
Ellis, Jack and Emma, 12
expropriation of Native resources, 1, 95n22
extinguishment bills, 2, 66–69, 74

Federal Land Policy Management Act, 55
fish camp of Kookwasx, 34
fishermen working a seine boat, 50
fishing and hunting rights, xxi, 3–4, 7, 28,
  91–92n4, 94n9
fishing industry, Alaska Natives and, 3
fishing regulations, federal, 49

fish traps, industrial, 3, 21, 25, 27–28, 49,
    59–60
Folta, George W., 55
Forest Service, 66–68
fox farm permits, 21, 102–103n56
Frazier, Lynn, 26

Glacier Bay, 5
Glacier Bay National Monument, 4, 39,
    97n27
Grant, Fred, 66
Gravel, Mike, 91n3
Great Depression, 35
Gruening, Ernest, 59, 86
    Alaska statehood and, xx, 57
    antireservation stance, 49–50, 71–73

*Haa Kusteeyí, Our Culture: Tlingit Life
    Stories* (Dauenhauer and Dauenhauer),
    13–14
Haida people, 15, 28, 30–31
    See also Central Council of Tlingit
        and Haida Indian Tribes of Alaska
        (CCTHITA); *Tlingit and Haida
        Indians of Alaska v. United States*
Haldane, George, 49
Hanna hearings (1944), 50, 102–103n56
Hanna Report (1945), 51
Hanna, Richard, 49–51
Haycox, Stephen
    on ANB, xix
    on CCTHITA, 41
    on Curry's questionable practices,
        109n87
    on Klukwan's rejection of reservation, 51
    on opposition to reserve concept, 49–50
    on pro-timber interests, 65–66
    on response to State of Alaska's
        disregard for Alaska Native claims,
        84–85
    on *Tlingit and Haida* judgment award
        process, 39–40
H.C.R. (House Concurrent Resolution)
    108, 62
health care, racial prejudice and
    discrimination in, 58
Hensley, Willie, 86, 118–119n187
Hoonah, Alaska, 69
Hope, Andrew "Andy" III, 29
    dedication, v
Hope, Andrew Percy, 9, 37, 56, 84
    elected to lead Tlingit-Haida Central
        Council, 36
    H.R. 1921, 80

response to judgment award in *Tlingit
    and Haida*, 39–40
Tongass Timber Act and, 66
Hope, Ishmael, 15–16, 101n40, 113n130
Hope, John, 37, 84
    on early ANB leaders, 15
    on history of ANB, 23, 99n36
    issue of representation in Washington,
        82
    William Paul to, 78, 116n166
    on rift between Andrew P. Hope and
        William Paul, Sr., 106n68
Hope, Percy, 84
Hopson, Eben, 56
Hotch Steve, 84
House Concurrent Resolution 108, 62
House Resolutions. *See* H.R. *entries*
Howard, Helen, 14
H.R. 206 (first Alaska statehood bill), 66
H.R. 331 (Alaska statehood bill), 69–73
H.R. 1921, 77–82, 116–117n166
H.R. 4388 (Possessory Claims Bill, Bartlett
    Land Bill, Alaska Native Claims Bill),
    75, 78
H.R. 7002 (extinguishment bill), 67–69
hunting and fishing rights, xxi, 3–4, 7, 28,
    91–92n4, 94n9
Hydaburg Indian Reservation, 45, 48, 51, 55

Ickes, Harold, 26, 45–46, 48–49, 70
Indian-chartered corporations, 30
Indian Citizenship Act of 1924 (Snyder
    Act), 96n25
Indian Reorganization Act, 1934 (IRA)
    (Wheeler-Howard Act)
    amendments to, 28–30, 45–46, 65
    Oscar Chapman to William Paul on
        councils formed by, 36
    James Curry on, 76
    extension of, to Alaska, 106n73
Indian reserves. *See* reservations (Indian
    reserves)
Indian Self-Determination and Education
    Assistance Act (1975), 96n25, 113n128
Indian tribes, legal and political status of,
    94n9
indigenous languages, 14, 98n34
IRA. *See* Indian Reorganization Act, 1934
    (IRA) (Wheeler-Howard Act)

Jackson, Henry "Scoop," 86
Jackson, Nathan, xii
Jackson, Sheldon, 13, 20, 46

Jacobs, Mark, Jr., 29
Jacobs, Mark, Sr., 84
Johnson (Tlingit chief), 103n57
Johnson, Frank G., 51, 54, 66, 72–73
Jones, C. F., 98n30
Juneau dance group, 72
Jurisdictional Act, 35
Jurisdictional Act (1935), 27–28, 30

Kahklen, Joe, Sr., 47–48
Kake reservation, proposed, 48
Karluk reservation, proposed, 48
Katanook, Eli, 13
Katlian, "Old Man Katlian," 14
Ketchikan Pulp and Paper Company, 66
Klawock reservation, 45, 48
Klukwan, rejection of reservation, 51
Kodiak Island reservation, proposed, 48
Koniag, Inc., xxii
koo.èex (potlatch), 101n39
Kookwasx, near her fish camp, 33
Krug, Julius "Cap," 51
Kuiu Island, 64

land
    "abandonment" of, 67, 69
    ANB's focus on obtaining
        compensation for lost rights and, 4,
        6, 48
    Bartlett Land Bill (H.R. 4388), 75, 78
    Federal Land Policy Management Act,
        55
    ownership of, in Pacific Northwest
        aboriginal cultures, 109n88
    reservations as means of reclaiming,
        51–52, 54
    terra nullius (land belonging to no one),
        xxiv, 95n22
    "use and occupancy" of, 8, 67–68, 69
    U.S. government's restrictive
        regulations on Alaska Natives' use
        and access to, 3–4
Langdon, Stephen, 2, 103n57, 112n105
Last Great Potlatch (1904), Sitka, 101n39
lawsuits against U.S. government, 8, 35, 65,
    104–105n57, 109n87
    See also Tee-Hit-Ton Indians v. United
        States; Tlingit and Haida Indians of
        Alaska v. United States
Lekanof, Flore, 86
Liberty, Paul, 13–14

Margold, Nathan, 26
Metcalfe, K. J., 111n103

Metcalfe, Vern, 100n39, 105n58, 105n60,
    106n68
Metlakatla, Annette Island Reserve, 44, 53
Meyer, Dillon S., 109n87
missionaries, American, 3
Mitchell, Donald Craig, 29, 31, 80, 103n57,
    107n78
Mt. Edgecumbe Hospital, flag raising, 42
Murkowski, Frank, 91n3
Murkowski, Lisa, 93n7

NANA Corporation, xxii
National Advisory Committee on Indian
    Affairs (NACIA), 68
National Congress of American Indians
    (NCAI), xix, 36–37, 65, 77–79
National Park Service, 5, 69
Native American Graves Protection and
    Repatriation Act of 1990 (NAGPRA),
    110n90
Native American tribes, xix–xx, 2, 25–26,
    28, 47
NCAI (National Congress of American
    Indians), xix, 36–37, 65, 77–79
Nelson Act, 18
Nichols, Philip, Jr., 40, 97n27
Nielson, Peter C., 77
North Slope Native Association, 85
Notti, Emil, 86, 87–88, 119n189
Nusunginya, John, 56

Office of Indian Affairs (OIA), 30–33, 35,
    46, 108n84
oil leases, 84–85, 86
Olson, Wallace M., 95n22
Organic Act (1884), 7
Organized Village of Kake v. Egan, 125

Paul, Frederick "Fred," 21, 31, 37, 77, 79
Paul, Louis, Jr., 20–21, 31
Paul, Louis, Sr., 20
Paul, Patrick, 82
Paul, Samuel, 20
Paul, Tillie, 20, 102n52
Paul, William, Jr. "Bill," 31, 37, 77–78, 79,
    79–80, 81
Paul, William, Sr., 6, 9, 32, 79
    aboriginal claims and, 8
    as Alaska Native rights advocate, 27
    ANB and, 20–21, 25, 82, 107n79
    animosity between Curry and, 115n153
    disbarment of, 31
    to John Hope, 116n166
    H.R. 1921 and, 80

H.R. 4388, 75–77
IRA amendments, 29–30
IRA extension to Alaska, 106n73
lawsuit against U.S. government, 35,
   104–105n57
as North Slope Native Association
   attorney, 85
OIA and, 31, 46
opposition to fish traps, 27
on Frank Peratrovich, 78
on pursuing claims as clans, 110n90
views on reservations, 6, 47, 50
voting templates, 102n55
See also Tee-Hit-Ton Indians v. United
   States
Peacock, J. C., 37–38, 82, 110n90
Peck, Cyrus, Sr., 84
Peratrovich, Elizabeth, 54, 59
as ANB liaison to NCAI, 78–79
and Anti-Discrimination Act, 59,
   116n165
opposition to H.R. 4388, 75–76
testimony of, before Congress, 113n130
Peratrovich, Frank, 31, 56, 57, 66, 78, 84, 84
Peratrovich, Roy, 31, 46, 54, 59, 75–76, 84,
   116n165
Perkins, Al, 29
Peterson, Helen, 79–82, 117n172
population, of Alaska and Alaska Natives, 57
Possessory Claims Bill (H.R. 4388), 75, 78
potlatch, 101n39
Pratt, Richard, 20
Presbyterian Church, 15, 17–18, 46, 98n30,
   98n33, 100n36
Price, Ralph, 15
Price, Robert, 30, 55, 97n27, 107n76
property rights, uncompensated taking of,
   4, 6, 67–68

Quinto, Marcello, *xii*

racial prejudice and discrimination, 57–59,
   101n49
Rayburn, Sam, 69–70
Reagan, Ronald, xx, 91n3
Regan, Kenneth, 110n90
reservations (Indian reserves)
ANB's perspective on, 45–47, 51–52,
   54, 70
Annette Island Reserve, 44, 46–48, 52,
   53, 71, 97n27
authorization for establishment by
   secretary of interior, 45–46, 48, 55, 65
debate over merits of, 6

Gruening's stance on, 49–50, 73
Klukwan's rejection of, 51
Native Americans and, 2, 52
opposition to, 54–55
proposed for Alaska Natives, 8–11, 45,
   48–49, 51–54
Rhoads, Charles, 26
Roosevelt, Franklin D., 10, 26
Roosevelt, Theodore, 3
Russian era in Alaska, 13–14, 98–99n34,
   100n38
Russian Orthodox Church, 13–14

salmon cannery interests, 50, 65
SCA (Sitka Community Association), 29
Sealaska Corporation, *xxii*
SEARHC (Southeast Alaska Regional
   Health Consortium), 42
seasonal rounds, modified, 16
self-determination of Alaska Natives, 15,
   46, 96n25, 113n128
Shakan, Prince of Wales Island, 16
Shales, Joyce Walton, 17–18
Simpson, Peter, 6
aboriginal claims and, 8
on Alaska Native land rights, 23
ANB Camp #1, 102n50
as "father of the ANB," 14–15
Native claims movement and, 99–
   100n36
suit against U.S. government, 104–
   105n57
Sitka Community Association (SCA), 29
Sitka School District, 18
Sitka Tribe of Alaska (Sitka Community
   Association), 29
Snyder Act (Indian Citizenship Act of
   1924), 96n25
Southeast Alaska Natives
AFN's inclusion of, in claims
   settlement, 87–88
reservations proposed for, 10–11, 49,
   52–54
views on reservations, 47
Southeast Alaska Regional Health
   Consortium (SEARHC), 42
Southeast Alaska timber industry, 64, 65, 75
Spanish expeditions to Alaska, 100n38
Stevens, Ted, 91n3
St. Gabriel's Brotherhood, 13
Strand, Martin, 101–102n50
subsistence rights, *xxi*, 7, 28, 69, 91–92n4,
   94n9
Sutherland, Dan, 23, 28, 47

Tamaree, Tillie Paul, 102n52
Tamaree, William, 20, 102n52
Tee-Hit-Ton Indians v. United States
    aboriginal title confirmed by, 8, 83
    ethnographic principle as basis for,
        37–38
    filed in U.S. Court of Claims, 37–38
    legal citation, 93–94n8, 125
    U.S. Court of Claims decision, 82
    U.S. Supreme Court decision, 38
termination movement, 60–63
terra nullius (land belonging to no one),
    xxiv, 95n22
Thomas, Edward K., 52, 60
Thomas, Margaret V., 107n79
timber industry, Southeast Alaska, 64, 65, 75
*Tlingit and Haida Indians of Alaska v. United
    States*
    aboriginal title validity established in, 8
    filed in U.S Court of Claims, 65
    findings by U.S. Court of Claims, 39,
        96–97n27
    judgment award, 39–40, 88
    Jurisdictional Act and, 30
    legal citation, 94n8, 125
    Bill Paul and, 79
Tlingit-Haida Central Council (Tlingit-
    Haida Claims Committee)
    lawsuit against U.S. government, 6–7,
        35, 65
    meeting in Wrangell (1941), 46
    OIA's response to formation of, 108n84
    See also Central Council of Tlingit
        and Haida Indian Tribes of Alaska
        (CCTHITA)
Tlingit people
    kwaan boundaries, 5
    organization of, 30–31
    population in 1900s, 15
    Presbyterian Church moral code vs.
        traditions of, 17–18
    right to pursue claims in U.S. Court of
        Claims, 28
    seal hunters, Glacier Bay, 5
Tongass National Forest, 4, 39, 76, 97n27
Tongass Timber Act (1947), 64, 66, 68
Trans-Alaska Pipeline, xx
treaties, aboriginal title and, 26, 88
treaties, with Native American tribes, 2
Treaty of Cession (1867), 7, 88, 95–96n23
tribal recognition, and aboriginal title, 1–2
tribal termination, in U.S. Indian policy, 62
Truman, Harry, 10, 68–69

Tsimshians of Metlakatla, and Annette
    Island Reserve, 71
tuberculosis epidemic, 58

Udall, Stewart, 85
uncompensated taking of property rights, 4,
    6, 67–68
U.S. Court of Claims
    Native American tribes' right to sue
        federal government in, 25–26, 28
    right of Tlingit people to pursue claims
        in, 28
    *See also Tee-Hit-Ton Indians v. United
        States; Tlingit and Haida Indians of
        Alaska v. United States*
"use and occupancy" of land, 8, 67–68, 69
user fees, for use of salmon streams, 2
U.S. government
    Alaska Natives' relationship with, 58
    Bureau of Indian Affairs, 30
    Department of Justice, 80
    disregard of Alaska Native claims, 21
    expropriation of Native resources, 1,
        95n22
    failure to recognize aboriginal title, 7
    fiduciary duty and trust responsibility
        of, 2
    Forest Service, 66–68
    lawsuits against, 8, 35, 65, 104–105n57,
        109n87 (*See also Tee-Hit-Ton Indians
        v. United States; Tlingit and Haida
        Indians of Alaska v. United States*)
    National Park Service, 5, 69
    Native American tribes' right to sue,
        25–26, 28
    Office of Indian Affairs (OIA), 30–33,
        35, 46, 108n84
    presumption of entitlement to Alaska, 26
    restrictive regulations on Alaska
        Natives' use of and access to land, 3
    threats to remove children, 16
    tribal termination, 62
    trust relationship with Native
        Americans, 113n128
    See also Department of the Interior

Van Ness, Bill, 41
Venetie reservation, proposed, 48
voting templates, 102n55

Walker, Norman "Doc," 59
Walton, Rudolph, 17–19
Weissbrodt, Israel "Lefty," 37, 39, 77

Wheeler-Howard Act. *See* Indian
    Reorganization Act, 1934 (IRA)
    (Wheeler-Howard Act)
Whitworth College, Tacoma, Washington,
    20
Wickersham, James
    aboriginal claims and, 8
    campaign for reelection as Alaska's
        congressional delegate, 25, 27, 105n58
    in lawsuit against U.S. government, 35,
        104–105n57
    William Paul and, 21
    recommendations of, at ANB 1929
        convention, 23–25
Wickites, 21
Widmark, Alfred, 82, *84*
Willard, James, *74*
Williams, Elizabeth, *84*
Williams, Joe, 77, *84*
Worl, Rosita, *xii*
Wright, Don, *86*
Wright, Ted, *29*

Young, Don, 91n3
Young, Ralph, 15

Zuboff, Cyril, *84*